BUDDHA

his life and teachings

OSHO

A BridgewaterBookCompany Book

First published in 2004

Book design © 2004 The Bridgewater Book Company Ltd.
Text © 2004 Osho International Foundation, www.osho.com

Paperback ISBN: 0-681-15316-4

Created and produced by The Bridgewater Book Company Ltd.
The Old Candlemakers
West Street
Lewes BN7 2NZ
UK

Creative Director: Terry Jeavons
Art Director: Sarah Howerd
Managing Editor: Mark Truman
Designer: Anna Hunter-Downing

Printed in China

The text material in this book is selected from various discourses by Osho
given to a live audience over a period of more than thirty years. All of the
Osho discourses have been published in full as books, and are also
available as original audio recordings. Audio recordings and the complete
text archive can be found via the online OSHO Library at www.osho.com

OSHO is a registered trademark of Osho International Foundation, used
with permission/license.

Picture acknowledgments
The publishers would like to thank the Osho International Foundation for
permission to reproduce the images on pp. 1, 2, 4, 5, 7, 8, 9, 10, 13, 14,
15, 17, 18, 21, 24, 25, 29, 32, 33, 35, 37, 39, 41, 42, 45, 48, 50, 51, 55, 57,
58, 61, 62, 63, 66, 68–69, 71, 75, 77, 79, 81, 82, 83, 85, 86, 89, 91, 94, 96,
99, 100, 101, 103, 104, 105, 107, 109, 112, 113, 115, 116, 117, 118, 121,
123, 125, 127, 131, 133, 135, 137, 139, 141, 142, 144.

The publishers would like to thank Leonard de Selva/Corbis for
permission to reproduce the image on p. 23.

contents

introduction

Gautam Buddha's given name was Siddhartha. Gautama is his family name so his full name was Gautama Siddhartha. Buddha is not his name, it is his awakening. Buddha simply means "one who is awakened." Gautam Buddha is the most famous awakened person but that does not mean that he is the only awakened person. There have been many buddhas before him and there have been many buddhas after him—and as long as every human being can become a buddha, new buddhas will go on springing up in the future. Everyone has the potentiality...it is only a matter of waiting for the right time. Some day, tortured by the outside reality, in despair of having seen everything and found nothing, you are bound to turn inward.

The very word *buddha* means "awakened intelligence." The word *buddhi*, "intellect," also comes from the same root. The root word *budh* has many dimensions to it. There is no single English word that can translate it. It has many implications; it is fluid and poetic. In no other language does any word like budh exist, with so many meanings. There are at least five meanings to the word *budh*.

The first is to awake, to wake oneself up, to awaken others, to be awake. As such, it is opposed to being asleep, in the slumber of delusion from which the enlightened awakens as from a dream. That is the first meaning of intelligence, budh: to create an awakening in you.

Ordinarily people are asleep. Even while you think you are awake, you are not. Walking on the road, you are fully awake—in your mind. But from the perspective of a buddha, you are fast asleep, because a thousand and one dreams and thoughts are clamoring inside you.

Your inner light is clouded in a kind of sleep. Yes, your eyes are open, obviously, but people can walk in a dream, in sleep, with open eyes. Buddha says you are also walking in sleep with open eyes.

But your inner eye is not open. You don't know yet who you are. You have not looked into your own reality. You are not awake. A mind full of thoughts is not awake, cannot be awake.

Only a mind that has dropped thoughts and thinking—which has dispersed the clouds so the sun is burning bright in a sky utterly empty of clouds—is the mind that is intelligent, that is awake.

Intelligence is the capacity to be in the present. The more you are in the past or in the future, the less intelligent you are. Intelligence is the capacity to be here now, to be in this moment and nowhere else. Then you are awake.

For example, you are sitting in a house and the house suddenly catches fire; your life is in danger. Then for a moment you will be awake. In that moment you will not think many thoughts. In that moment you forget your past. In that moment you will not be clamored at by your psychological memories: that you had loved a woman thirty years before, and boy, it was fantastic! Or that the other day you had been to the Chinese restaurant, and still the taste lingers with the aroma of the freshly cooked food. You will not be in those thoughts. No, when your house is on fire you cannot afford this kind of thinking. Suddenly you will rush to this moment: the house is on fire and your life is at stake. You will not dream about the future or about what you are going to do tomorrow. Tomorrow is no longer relevant, yesterday is no longer relevant—even today is no longer relevant! Only this moment, this split second.

That is the first meaning of budh, intelligence. And then there are great insights. A man who wants to be awake, wants to be a buddha, has to live each moment in such intensity as you live only rarely—rarely, in some danger. The first meaning is the opposite of sleep. Naturally, you can see reality only when you are not asleep. You can face it, you

can look into the eyes of truth—or call it "God"—only when you are awake. Do you understand the point of intensity, the point of being on fire? Utterly awake, there is insight. That insight brings freedom; that insight brings truth.

The second meaning of budh is to recognize, to become aware of, acquainted with, to notice, give heed to. A buddha is one who has recognized the false as the false, and has opened his eyes to the true as the true. To see the false as false is the beginning of understanding what truth is. Only when you see the false as false can you see what truth is. You cannot go on living in illusions; you cannot go on living in your beliefs; you cannot go on living in your prejudices if you want to know truth. The false has to be recognized as false. That is the second meaning of budh—recognition of the false as false, of the untrue as untrue.

For example, you have believed in God; you were born a Christian or a Hindu or a Mohammedan. You have been taught that God exists, you have been made afraid of God—if you don't believe in him you will suffer, you will be punished. God is ferocious; he will never forgive you. The Jewish God says, "I am a jealous God. Worship only me and nobody else!" The

Mohammedan God says the same thing: "There is only one God, and no other God; and there is only one prophet of God, Mohammed, and no other prophet."

This conditioning can go so deep in you that it can linger even if you start disbelieving in God.

You have been brought up to believe in God, and you have believed. This is a belief. Whether God actually exists or not has nothing to do with your belief. Truth has nothing to do with your belief! Whether you believe or not makes no difference to truth. But if you believe in God you will go on seeing—at least thinking that you see—God. If you don't believe in God, that disbelief in God will prevent you from knowing. All beliefs prevent you because they become prejudices around you, they become "thought-coverings"—what Buddha calls *avarnas*.

The man of intelligence does not believe in anything and does not *disbelieve* in anything The man of intelligence is open to recognizing whatsoever is the case. If God is there he will recognize—but not according to his belief. He has no belief.

Only in a nonbelieving intelligence can truth appear. When you already believe, you don't allow truth any space to come to you. Your prejudice is already enthroned. You cannot see something that goes against your belief; you will become afraid, you will become shaky, you will start trembling. You have put so much into your belief— so much life, so much time, so many prayers, five prayers every day. For fifty years a man has been devoted to his belief—now, suddenly, how can he recognize the fact that there is no God? A man has put his whole life into communism, believing that there is no God; how can he come to see if God is there? He will go on avoiding.

I'm not saying anything about whether God exists or is not. What I am saying is something concerned with you, not with God. A clear mind is needed, an intelligence is needed that does not cling to any belief. Then you are like a mirror: you reflect that which is; you don't distort it.

That is the second meaning of *budh*. An intelligent person is neither a communist nor a Catholic. An intelligent person does not believe, does not disbelieve. That is not his way. He looks into life and whatsoever is there he is ready to see it. He has no barriers to his vision; his vision is transparent. Only those few people attain to truth.

The third meaning of the root *budh*, intelligence, is to know, to understand. Buddha knows that which is; he understands that which is, and in that very understanding he is free from all bondage. Budh means to know in the sense of to *understand*, not in the sense of knowledgeability. Buddha is not knowledgeable. An intelligent person does not care much about information and knowledge. An intelligent person cares much more for the capacity to know. His authentic interest is in knowing, not in knowledge.

Knowing gives you understanding; knowledge only gives you a feeling of understanding without giving you *real* understanding. Knowledge is a false coin; it is deceptive. It only gives you the feeling that you know, yet you don't know at all. You can accumulate knowledge as much as you want, you can go on hoarding, you can become extremely knowledgeable. You can write books, you can have degrees, you can have PhDs and LittDs, and still you remain the same ignorant, stupid person you have always been. Those degrees don't change you; they *can't* change you. In fact, your stupidity becomes stronger; it has degrees now! It can prove itself through certificates. It cannot prove itself through life, but it can prove itself through the certificates. It cannot prove anything in any other way, but it will carry degrees, certificates, recognitions from society. People think you know, and you also think you know.

Have you not seen this? The people who are thought to be very knowledgeable are as ignorant as anybody, sometimes more ignorant. It is rare to find intelligent people in the academic world, very rare. I have been in the academic world and I say it through my own experience. I have seen intelligent farmers, but I have not seen intelligent professors. I have seen intelligent woodcutters, but I have not seen intelligent professors. Why? What has gone wrong with these people?

One thing has gone wrong: they can depend on knowledge. They need not become knowers, they can depend on knowledge. They have found a secondhand way. The firsthand needs courage. The firsthand, knowing, only a few people can afford—the adventurers, people who go beyond the ordinary path where crowds move, people who take small footpaths into the jungle of the unknowable. The

danger is that they may get lost. The risk is high. When you can get secondhand knowledge, why bother? You can just sit in your chair. You can go to the library or to the university, you can collect information. You can make a big pile of information and sit on top of it.

Through knowledge your memory becomes bigger and bigger, but your intelligence does not become bigger. Sometimes it happens when you don't know much, when you are not very knowledgeable, that you will have to be intelligent.

I have heard…

A woman bought a tin of fruit but she could not open the tin. She did not know how to open it, so she rushed to her study to look in a cookbook. By the time she looked in the book and found the page and reference, and came rushing back ready to open the tin, the servant had already opened it.

She asked, "But how did you do it?"

The servant said, "Madam, when you can't read, you have to use your mind."

Yes, that's how it happens! That's why illiterate farmers, gardeners, woodcutters, are more intelligent, have a kind of freshness around them. They can't read, so they have to use their minds. One has to live and one has to use one's mind.

The third meaning of budh is to know, in the sense of understanding. The Buddha has seen that which is. He understands that which is, and in that very understanding he is free from all bondage.

What does it mean? If you want to get rid of fear you will have to understand fear. But if you want to avoid the fact that fear is there, that the fear of death is there…if you are afraid inside, you will have to create something strong around you like a hard shell, so nobody comes to know that you are afraid. And that is not the only point—you also will not know that you are afraid because of that hard shell. It will protect you from others and it will protect you from your own understanding.

An intelligent person does not escape from any fact. If it is fear he will go into it, because the way out is through. If he feels fear and trembling arising in him, he will leave everything else aside: first this fear has to be gone through. He will go into it; he

will try to understand. He will not try to figure out how not to be afraid; he will not ask that question. He will simply ask one question: "What is this fear? It is there, it is part of me, it is my reality. I have to go into it, I have to understand it. If I don't understand it then a part of me will always remain unknown to me. And how am I going to know who I am if I go on avoiding parts of myself? I will not understand fear, I will not understand death, I will not understand anger. I will not understand my hatred, I will not understand my jealousy, I will not understand this and that...."

Then how are you going to know yourself? All these things are you! This is your being. You have to go into everything that is there, every nook and corner. You have to explore fear. Even if you are trembling it is nothing to be worried about: tremble, but go in. It is far better to tremble than to escape, because once you escape, that part will remain unknown to you. And you will become more and more afraid to look at it, because that fear will go on accumulating. It will become bigger and bigger if you don't go into it right now, this moment. Tomorrow it will have lived twenty-four hours more. Beware!—it will have grown more roots in you, it will have bigger foliage, it will have become stronger, and then it will be more difficult to tackle. It is better to go right now. It is already late.

Go into it and see it.... And seeing means without prejudice. Seeing means that you don't condemn fear as bad from the very beginning. Who knows?—it is not bad—who knows that it is? The explorer has to remain open to all the possibilities; he cannot afford a closed mind. A closed mind and exploration don't go together. He will go into it. If it brings suffering and pain, he will suffer the pain but he will go into it. Trembling, hesitant, but he will go into it: "It is my territory,

I have to know what it is. Maybe it is carrying some treasure for me? Maybe the fear is only there to protect the treasure."

That's my experience; that's my understanding: If you go deep into your fear you will find love. That's why it happens that when you are in love, fear disappears. And when you are afraid, you cannot be in love. What does this mean? A simple arithmetic—fear and love don't exist together. That means it must be the same energy that becomes fear; then there is nothing left to become love. It becomes love; then there is nothing left to become fear.

Go into each negative thing and you will find the positive. And knowing the negative and the positive, the third, the ultimate happens—the transcendental. That is the meaning of understanding, *budh*, intelligence.

The fourth meaning is to be enlightened and to enlighten. The Buddha is the light; he has become the light. And since he's the light and he has become the light, he shows the light to others, too—naturally, obviously. He is illumination. His darkness has disappeared; his inner flame is burning bright. Smokeless is his flame. This meaning is opposed to darkness and the corresponding blindness and ignorance. This is the fourth meaning: to become light, to become enlightened.

Ordinarily you are a darkness, a continent of darkness, a dark continent, unexplored. People are a little strange: they go on exploring the Himalayas, they go on exploring the Pacific, they go on reaching for the moon and Mars; there is just one thing they never try—exploring the inner being. Humankind has landed on the moon, but people have not landed yet in their own beings. This is strange. Maybe landing on the moon is just an escape, going to Everest is just an escape. Maybe he does not want to go inside because he's very much afraid. He substitutes with some other explorations to feel good; otherwise, he will have to feel guilty. You start climbing a mountain and you feel good—but the greatest mountain is within you and is yet unclimbed! You start diving deep into the Pacific, but the greatest Pacific is within you and uncharted, unmapped. And you start going to the moon—what foolishness! You are wasting your energy in going to the moon, when the real moon is within you—because the real light is within you.

The intelligent person will go inward first. Before going anywhere else, you will go into your own being. That is the first thing, and it should have the first preference. Only when you have known yourself can you go anywhere else. Then wherever you go you will carry a blissfulness around you, a peace, a silence, a celebration.

The fourth meaning is to be enlightened. Intelligence is the spark. Helped, cooperated with, it can become the fire and the light and the warmth. It can become light, it can become life, it can become love—those are all included in the word *enlightenment*. An enlightened person has no dark corners in his being. All is like the morning—the sun is on the horizon, the darkness and the dismalness of the night have disappeared, and the shadows of the night have disappeared. The earth is again awake. To be a buddha is to attain to a morning, a dawn within you. That is the function of intelligence, the ultimate function.

The fifth meaning of budh is to fathom. A depth is there in you, a bottomless depth, which has to be fathomed. The fifth meaning can also be to penetrate, to drop all that obstructs and penetrate to the core of your being.

People try to penetrate many things in life. Your urge, your desire for sex is nothing but a kind of penetration. But that is a penetration into the other. The same penetration has to happen into your own being—you have to penetrate yourself. If you penetrate somebody else it can give you a momentary glimpse, but if you penetrate yourself you can attain to the universal, cosmic orgasm that remains and remains and remains.

A man meets an outer woman, and a woman meets an outer man: this is a very superficial meeting—yet meaningful, yet it brings moments of joy. But when the inner woman meets the inner man.... And you are carrying both inside you: a part of you is feminine, a part of you is masculine. Whether you are man or woman does not matter; everybody is bisexual. The fifth meaning of the root budh is penetration. When your inner man penetrates your inner woman there is a meeting; you become whole, you become one. All desires for the outer disappear. In that desirelessness is freedom, nirvana.

The path of Buddha is the path of budh. Remember that "Buddha" is not the name of Gautama the Buddha; Buddha is the state that he has attained. His name was Gautama Siddhartha. Then one day he became Buddha, one day his *bodhi*, his intelligence, bloomed. "Buddha" means exactly what "Christ" means. Jesus' name is not Christ;

that is the ultimate flowering that happened to him. So it is with Buddha. There have been many buddhas other than Gautama Siddhartha.

Everybody has the capacity for budh. But budh, that capacity to see, is just like a seed in you—if it sprouts, becomes a big tree, blooms, starts dancing in the sky, starts whispering to the stars, you are a buddha.

The path of Buddha is the path of intelligence. It is not an emotional path, no, not at all. Not that emotional people cannot reach; there are other paths for them—the path of devotion, *Bhakti Yoga*. Buddha's path is pure *Gyan Yoga*, the path of knowing. Buddha's path is the path of meditation, not of love.

The intellect has to be used, not discarded; it has to be transcended, not discarded. It can be transcended only when you have reached the uppermost rung of the ladder. You have to go on growing in intelligence. Then a moment will come when intelligence has done all that it can do. In that moment, say goodbye to intelligence. It has helped you a long way, it has brought you far enough, it has been a good vehicle. It has been a boat you crossed with; you have reached the other shore, then you leave the boat. You don't carry the boat on your head; that would be foolish.

Buddha's path goes through intelligence and goes beyond it. A moment comes when intelligence has given you all that it can give, then it is no longer needed. Then finally you drop it, too; its work is finished. The disease is gone, now the medicine has to go, too When you are free of the disease and the medicine, too, only then are you free. Sometimes it happens that the disease is gone, but you have become addicted to the medicine. This is not freedom. A thorn is in your foot and is hurting. You take another thorn so that the thorn in your foot can be taken out with the help of the other. When you have taken the thorn out, you throw away both; you don't save the one that has been helpful. It is now meaningless.

The work of intelligence is to help you to become aware of your being. Once that work has happened and your being is there, there is no need for this instrument. You can say goodbye, you can say thank you. Buddha's path is the path of intelligence, pure intelligence, although it goes beyond it.

the birth of an
emperor

These beautiful metaphors have to be understood with great sympathy, with great intuitiveness, with love, poetry. Not with logic; otherwise you will destroy them.

buddha's arrival

Every human being is born to be a Buddha; every person has the seed of buddhahood within. If you look at the masses, it doesn't seem to be true. If it were true, there would be many buddhas—but one rarely hears about a buddha. We only know that somewhere, twenty-five centuries ago, a certain Siddhartha Gautama became Buddha. Who knows whether it is true or not? It may be a myth, a beautiful story, a consolation, an opiate for the masses to keep them hoping that one day they will also become buddhas. Who knows whether Buddha is an historic reality?

S O MANY STORIES have been woven around Buddha that he looks more like a mythological figure than a reality. When he becomes enlightened, gods come from heaven, play beautiful music, and dance around him. Now, how can this be historical? Flowers shower on him from the sky—flowers of gold and silver, flowers of diamonds and emeralds. Who can believe that this is historical?

This is not history, true—I agree. This is poetry. But it symbolizes something historical, because something so unique has happened in Buddha that there is no other way to describe it than to bring poetry in. Real flowers have not showered on Buddha, but whenever somebody becomes enlightened the whole existence rejoices—because we are not separate from it. When you have a headache your whole body suffers, and when the headache goes away, your whole body feels good, feels a sense of well being. We are not separate from existence. Until you are a buddha you are a headache— a headache to yourself, a headache to others, a headache to existence. You are a thorn in the flesh of existence. When the headache disappears, when the thorn becomes a flower, when one person becomes a buddha, a great pain that he was creating for himself and others disappears. Certainly—I vouch for it, I am a witness to it—certainly the whole of existence rejoices, dances, sings. But how to describe it? It is nothing visible; photographs cannot be taken of it. Hence the poetry; hence these metaphors, symbols, similes.

It is said that when Buddha was born his mother immediately died. It may not be a historical fact or it may be. But my feeling is that it is not a historical fact, because it is said that whenever a buddha is born, the mother immediately dies, and that is not true. There have been many buddhas—Jesus' mother did not die, Mahavira's mother did not die, Krishna's mother did not die. Maybe Siddhartha Gautama's mother died, but it cannot be said that whenever a buddha is born the mother dies, not historically.

But I know it has some significance of its own that is not historical. By the "mother" is not really meant the mother; by the "mother" is meant your past. You are reborn when you become a buddha; your past functions as a womb, as the mother. The moment a buddha is born, the moment you become enlightened, your past dies. That death is necessary. This is absolutely true. It happened with Mahavira, with Krishna, with Jesus; it has always happened. To communicate it, it is said that whenever a buddha is born the mother dies. You will have to be sympathetic to understand these things.

I can understand that it is difficult, looking at the greater part of humanity, to see that there is any possibility of every human being becoming a Christ or a Buddha. Looking at a seed, can you believe that one day it can become a lotus? Just looking at the seed, dissecting the seed, can you conclude that this seed is going to become a lotus? There seems to be no relationship at all. The seed looks like nothing, and when you dissect it you find nothing in it, only emptiness. Still, each seed carries a lotus within it—and each human being carries the buddha within.

When Buddha was born, it is said that a great sage, one hundred and twenty years old, immediately rushed from the Himalayas. His disciples asked, "Where are you going?" He ran! They had rarely even seen him walk, because he was so old. And he didn't answer them because there was no time; he just said, "No time to answer."

ENLIGHTENED INNOCENCE

The story is that Gautam Buddha was born while his mother was standing under a saal tree. And not only that, he was born standing. The first thing he did was to take seven steps in front of his mother and declare to the universe, "I am the most enlightened person ever."

In fact, every newborn child, if he could, would say the same thing, "I am enlightened." If every newborn child could walk, he would take seven steps and declare to the whole world, "I am the most enlightened person, unique."

Perhaps the story is a symbolic way of recognizing each child's innocence as his enlightenment, as his ultimate experience.

The disciples followed the old sage down into the plains. Buddha was born close to the Himalayas, on the border of Nepal and India. The old man immediately went to the king's palace. The king could not believe his eyes, because this man was not known to go anywhere. For at least fifty years he had lived in a single cave. Buddha's father could not believe it. He touched the old man's feet and said, "Why have you come? What has happened?"

The old man said, "I don't have much time, because my death is approaching. That's why I had to run. Where is your child? I have come to see him."

Buddha was just one day old. The moment he was born this old man had started running; it took twenty-four hours for him to reach the plains. The king could not believe it, because this old man was famous, a Master of Masters—why should he be interested in his child?

The child was brought immediately, and the old man, one hundred and twenty years old, touched Buddha's feet and started crying. The father was puzzled, the mother was shocked. "Why is he crying? Is there something wrong?" They asked him, "Why are you crying? Isn't the child going to survive? Is there going to be some calamity? Say it clearly—why are you crying?"

He said, "No, I am not crying because of any calamity. I am crying for joy because I have seen, and I am crying also because I will not live to see the full flowering of this man. I have seen him only in the bud, but even that is too much, to see a buddha in the bud. I am crying for joy, because a god is born! I am also crying in sadness because I will not be able to see him grow; my days are numbered. Soon I will be leaving my body; I will not be able to see what flowering he brings to the world, what fragrance he brings to the world. Millions and millions of people will become enlightened because of him. He has brought a light; he has brought a revolution into the world.... But don't be worried; be happy, rejoice!"

These are parables. These events may not have happened historically, but history is not our concern at all. Our concern is something more important, more essential, more eternal. History is a procession of events in time. Even if it did not happen historically, it doesn't matter; the parable is beautiful: a one-hundred-twenty-year-old saint bowing down to one-day-old Buddha. Age does not matter; awareness has no age. Ordinary formalities have to be dropped. The old man touching the feet of a child, a one-day-old child, crying for joy—those who understand will always cry for joy whenever they see something of immense value happening in the world.

But few will be able to see—even the father had not seen, the mother had not seen. Only those who have eyes will be able to see. The three wise men from the East had to travel thousands of miles to see, but the people of Jesus' own country could not see. Jesus' parents had to escape from Jerusalem; they had to escape to Egypt. And Jesus could not appear back in Jerusalem. After thirty years we hear of him again, and then he could survive only three years. The people of his own country killed him. Blind people killed the man who had eyes; mad people killed one of the sanest men.

Even the parents... Jesus' parents were not aware of what had happened. Three men from the East were needed to recognize him. Only those who have learned something of meditation will be able to recognize a buddha. When you come across a buddha it is not easy to recognize him. It is easy to be antagonized, it is easy to be angered; it is easy to be offended by his presence because his presence makes you feel so small that it offends you. His presence makes you feel so empty that it humiliates you—not that he means any humiliation, but because of your ego you start feeling humiliated. Your mind wants to take revenge. That's why Socrates was poisoned,

Mansoor was killed, Jesus was crucified—and it has always been so. Whenever there has been a buddha, the society has been very inimical toward him.

Even in India, even in the East, the same thing happened. Buddha lived in India,

> *When you come across a buddha it is not easy to recognize him*

preached there, transformed thousands of people into a world of light, but Buddhism disappeared from India. It was destroyed. After Buddha died, within five hundred years the religion was uprooted from there. The Brahmins did not like the idea; the pundits, the scholars did not like the idea—it was dangerous to their profession. If Buddha is right, then all the priests are wrong.

But, remember, these beautiful metaphors have to be understood with great sympathy, with great intuitiveness, with love, poetry. Not with logic; otherwise, you will destroy them; you will kill them. Sometimes beautiful metaphors have been used…and the religions, the so-called religions, the followers, have killed these metaphors themselves.

It is said that whenever Mohammed moved in the desert, a cloud would move just over his head to shelter him. Now, to be in the Arabian deserts is to be in fire! It is not a historical fact. No cloud will do this. Even human beings don't understand Mohammed—how will the poor cloud understand Mohammed? People were after Mohammed; his whole life he was escaping from one town to another town. His whole life he was always in danger, his survival was always in question. When men were not able to understand him, how could a poor cloud understand him? So it can't be historical. But still I love it—the metaphor is beautiful. The metaphor simply says that clouds are far more intelligent than humans; it says that even clouds understood the beauty of the man and protected him, even against the laws of nature. Wherever Mohammed was going they would go; even if the wind was not going there, the cloud would go on sheltering him. It shows that the ignorance of humanity is so great that even clouds are far more intelligent.

It is said that whenever Buddha came and wherever he moved, trees would bloom out of season, trees that had been long dead would again start sprouting green leaves. Beautiful poetry, significant poetry, lovely poetry to be meditated upon—I don't think it is historical, but it is still significant. It may not be a fact, but it is a truth.

Facts belong to ordinary events. The fact is that Buddha's own cousin, Devadatta, tried to kill him in many ways. Once when Buddha was meditating, Devadatta threw a rock at him from the top of a hill; a great rock started rolling downward. This is a fact—Devadatta tried to kill Buddha because he could not believe it: "How can Buddha become enlightened? We have played together; we have always been together in our childhood; we were educated together. If I am not enlightened, how is he enlightened?"

Devadatta declared himself enlightened, although he was not. And he would have been accepted as enlightened if Buddha had not been there. But how can you declare your unenlightened being to be enlightened in the presence of a Buddha? It was impossible. The only problem was how to destroy Buddha. He released a rock. The story goes that the rock came close to Buddha and then changed its course. That cannot be a fact, but it is a truth. Truth is a much higher phenomenon.

Devadatta released a mad elephant to kill Buddha. The mad elephant came ferociously, but when he reached Buddha, he looked at him and he bowed down and touched his feet. That Devadatta released a mad elephant is a fact; that it bowed to Buddha is not a fact. That is poetry, sheer poetry—but of immense truth.

Remember, scriptures talk about truth; they are not history books. History books talk about facts. That's why in history books you will find Alexander the Great, Ivan the Terrible, Adolf Hitler, and all kinds of neurotics. But Buddha, Mahavira, Jesus…they are not part of the history books. For them we need a totally different approach. It is good they are not part of history books, for they are not part of history; they come from the beyond; they belong to the beyond. They are only for those who are ready to rise and soar to the beyond.

The day Buddha was born—he was the son of a great king, the only son, and he was born when the king was getting old, very old—there was great rejoicing in the kingdom. The people had waited long. The king was much loved by the people; he had served them, he had been kind and compassionate, he had been loving and sharing. He had made his kingdom one of the richest, loveliest kingdoms of those days.

People were praying that their king should have a son because there was nobody to inherit. Then Buddha was born in the king's very old age—unexpected was his birth. There was great celebration, great rejoicing! All the astrologers of the kingdom gathered to make predictions about Buddha. He was given the name Siddhartha, because it means fulfillment. The king was fulfilled, his desire was fulfilled, his deepest longing was fulfilled. He had wanted a son his whole life; hence the name Siddhartha. It simply means "fulfillment of the deepest desire."

This son made the king's life meaningful, significant. The great astrologers made predictions—and they were all in agreement except for one young astrologer. His name was Kodanna. The king had asked, "What is going to happen in the life of my son?" And all the astrologers raised two fingers, except Kodanna, who raised only one finger.

The king said, "Please don't talk in symbols—I am a simple man, I don't know anything about astrology. Tell me, what do you mean by two fingers?"

And they all said, "Either he is going to become a *chakravartin*—a world ruler—or he will renounce the world and will become a buddha, an enlightened person. These two alternatives are there; hence, we raise two fingers."

The king was worried about the second alternative, that his son would renounce the world, so again the problem would arise. "Who will inherit my kingdom if he renounces the world?" He asked Kodanna, "Why do you raise only one finger?"

Kodanna said, "I am absolutely certain that he will renounce the world—he will become a buddha, an enlightened one, an awakened one."

The king was not happy with Kodanna. Truth is very difficult to accept. He ignored Kodanna and did not reward him at all—truth is not rewarded in this world. On the contrary, truth is punished in a thousand and one ways. In fact, Kodanna's prestige fell after that day. Because the king did not reward him, the rumor spread that he was a fool. When all the other astrologers were in agreement, he was the only one who was not.

The king asked the other astrologers, "What do you suggest? What should I do so that he does not renounce the world? I would not want him to be a beggar, I would not like to see him a monk, a *sannyasin*. I would like him to become a *chakravartin*—a ruler of all six continents." This is the ambition of all parents. Who would like their son or daughter to renounce the world and to move into the mountains, to go into their own inner world to seek and search for the self? Our desires are for external things. The king was an ordinary man, just like everybody else, with the same desires and the same ambitions.

The astrologers said, "It can be arranged. Give him as much pleasure as possible, keep him in as much comfort and luxury as is humanly possible. Don't allow him to know about illness, old age, and particularly death. Don't let him come to know about death and he will never renounce."

They were right in a way, because death is the central question. Once it arises in your heart, your lifestyle is bound to change. You cannot go on living in the old foolish way. If this life is going to end in death, then this life cannot be the real life; this life must be an illusion. Truth has to be eternal if it is true—only lies are momentary. If life is momentary, then it must be an illusion, a lie, a misconception, a misunderstanding; then our conception of life must be rooted somewhere in ignorance. We must be living it in such a way that it comes to an end. We can live in a different way so that we can become part of the eternal flow of existence.... Only death can give you that radical shift. So the astrologers said, "Please don't let him know anything about death."

The king made all the arrangements. He made three palaces for Siddhartha for different seasons, in different places, so that he would never come to know the discomforts of the seasons. When it was hot he had a palace in the hills where it was always cool. When it was cold he had another palace by the side of a river where it was always warm. The king made all the arrangements so Siddhartha never felt any discomfort.

No old man or woman was allowed to enter the palaces where he lived—only young people. He gathered all the beautiful young women of the kingdom around so that Siddhartha would remain allured, fascinated, so he would remain in dreams, desires. A sweet dream world was created for him. The gardeners were told that dead leaves had to be removed in the night; fading, withering flowers had to be removed in the night—because who knows? Seeing a dead leaf, the boy might start asking about what happened to this leaf, and the question of death could arise. Seeing a withering rose, petals falling, he might ask, "What has happened to this rose?" and he might start brooding, meditating, about death.

He was kept absolutely unaware of death for twenty-nine years. But how long can you avoid it? Death is such an important phenomenon. How long can you deceive a person? Sooner or later he had to enter into the world. Now the king was getting older and the son had to know the ways of the world. Gradually he was allowed out, but whenever he would pass through any street of the capital, the old men and women would be removed. Beggars would be removed. No *sannyasin* was allowed to appear while he was passing by, because seeing a *sannyasin* he might ask, "What type of man is this? Why is he in ochre robes? What has happened to him? Why does he look different, detached, distant? His eyes are different, his flavor is different, his presence has a different quality to it. What has happened to this man?" And then the question of renunciation would arise, and fundamentally the question of death....

But one day, it had to happen. It couldn't be avoided. One day Siddhartha had to become aware, and he became aware. The prince, of course, was supposed to inaugurate the yearly youth festival. It was a beautiful evening; the youth of the kingdom had gathered to dance and sing and rejoice the whole night. The first day of the year—a nightlong celebration and Siddhartha was going to open it.

On the way he met what his father had been afraid of him ever seeing—he came across those things....

coming of age

THE STORY is beautiful. From here it becomes mythological, but still it is significant.

The story goes that Indra, who was the chief of all the gods, became worried that a man who was capable of becoming enlightened was being distracted. Something had to be done; existence should not be allowed to miss an enlightened being. So it is said that Indra took a few gods with him to earth.

The street was always cleared when Siddhartha passed, so it was impossible for any person to enter there. Only gods could enter— that's why they had to create the mythology— because gods are invisible yet they can become visible any moment.

First a god, sick and feverish, passed by the chariot. If the street had been full of traffic, perhaps Siddhartha would have missed seeing him. But the street was empty, the houses were empty; there were no other vehicles, only his golden chariot. Siddhartha saw this man trembling, and he asked his charioteer, "What has happened to this man?"

Now, the man who was driving the chariot was in a dilemma because the orders of the king were that this young man should not know that anybody ever gets sick. This man was so sick that it seemed as if he was going to fall down right there and die. But Indra was determined. He forced the charioteer to tell the truth—"because

ultimately your commitment is not toward that old king, your commitment is toward truth. Don't miss this point, because this man is going to become an enlightened one, and you will be immensely blessed because you will be the cause of triggering the process. Don't miss it— you may not find it again in millions of lives."

Of course it was clear. The charioteer said, "I am not supposed to say this, but how can I lie to you? The truth is that before this, all people have been removed from the streets where you travel. I wonder where this man has come from, because everywhere there are guards and the army. Nobody is allowed to enter the path where the chariot is moving. This man is sick."

Siddhartha asked, "What is sickness?"

The charioteer explained, "Sickness is something we are born with, we are carrying all kinds of sickness in the body. Sometimes, in a certain situation, a weakness that you are carrying within you gets support from the outside and you get an infection, you become sick."

Then an old man appeared, another god, almost a hunchback, so old that Siddhartha could not believe his eyes: "What has happened to this man?" The charioteer said, "This is what happens after many sicknesses…this man has become old."

And then, a dead body—another god posing as a dead body—came by, with four

OBSERVE THE SETTING SUN

Buddha chose for his *sannyasins* the yellow robe. Yellow represents death, the yellow leaf. Yellow represents the setting sun, the evening. Buddha emphasized death, and it helps in a way. People become more and more aware of life in contrast to death. When you emphasize death again and again and again, you help people to awaken; they have to be awake because death is coming. Whenever Buddha would initiate a new sannyasin, he would tell him, "Go to the cemetery: just be there and watch funeral pyres, dead bodies being carried and burned...go on watching. And remember that this is going to happen to you, too." Three months' meditation on death, then coming back—that was the beginning of *sannyas*.

gods carrying him on a stretcher. Siddhartha asked, "What is happening?"

The charioteer said, "This man is at the last stage. After that old man, this is what happens."

Siddhartha said, "Stop the chariot here and answer me truthfully: Is all this going to happen to me too?"

At that moment he saw a monk, another god pretending to be a monk. Siddhartha said, "And what stage is this? With a shaven head, a staff in his hand, a begging bowl..."

The charioteer said, "This is not a stage like the others; this is a type of person who has become aware of life's misery, suffering, anguish, sickness, old age, death. He has dropped out of life and is in search of truth, in search of finding something that is immortal—the deathless, the truth."

Siddhartha said, "Return to the house. I have become sick, sick unto death. I have become old, old even though to all appearances I am young. What does it matter if old age is a few years

ahead of me, soon it is going to be walking by my side! I don't want to be like that dead man. Although I am alive for all ordinary purposes, I died with that dead man. Death is going to come; it is only a question of time, a question of sooner or later. It can come tomorrow or years from tomorrow; anyway, some day it is going to happen."

He said, "Tonight keep the chariot ready. I am going to be the last type of man. I am renouncing all that I have. I have not found happiness here. I will seek it, I will pursue it, I will do everything that is needed to find happiness."

What the astrologers had suggested to Buddha's father had looked like common sense...but common sense is superficial. They could not figure out one simple thing: that you cannot keep a man for his whole life unaware of reality. It is better to let him know from the beginning; otherwise, it will come as a big explosion in his life.

And that's what happened.

All the commentaries have said that Buddha renounced the world. It is not true. The world simply fell away; it ceased to have any meaning for him.

The night he moved away from his palace to the mountains, when he was crossing the boundary of his kingdom, his charioteer tried to convince him to go back to the palace. The charioteer was an old man. He had known Buddha from his childhood; he was almost the same age as Buddha's father. He said, "What are you doing? This is sheer madness. Have you gone insane or what? Look back!"

It was a full-moon night and his marble palace looked so beautiful. In the light of the full moon, the white marble of his palace was a joy to see. People used to come from faraway places just to have a glimpse of Buddha's palace in the full moon, just as people go to see the Taj Mahal. White marble has a tremendous beauty when the moon is full. There is synchronicity between the full moon and white marble, a certain harmony, a rhythm, a communion. The charioteer said, "Look back at least once to your beautiful palace. Nobody else has such a beautiful palace."

Buddha looked back and told the old man, "I don't see any palace there but only a great fire. The palace is on fire, only flames. Simply leave me here and go back; if you see the palace, go back to the palace. I don't see any palace there, because death is coming closer every moment. And I don't see any palace there

because all palaces disappear sooner or later. In this world, everything is momentary and I am in search of the eternal. Seeing the momentariness of this world, I can no longer fool myself."

These are his exact words, "I cannot fool myself anymore."

Not that he is renouncing the world! What can he do? If you see something as rubbish, if you see that the stones that you have carried all this time are not real diamonds, what are you going to do with them? It will not need great courage to drop them, to throw them away. It will not need great intelligence to get rid of them—they will immediately fall from your hands. You were not clinging to those stones, but to the idea that they were diamonds. You were clinging to your fallacy, your illusion.

Buddha has not renounced the world, he has renounced his illusions about it. And that, too, was a *happening*, not an act. When renunciation comes as a happening it has a tremendous beauty, because there is no motive in it. It is not a means to gain something else. It is total. You are finished with desiring, you are finished with the future, you are finished with power, money, and prestige, because you have seen the futility of it all.

awakening at bodhgaya

FOR SIX YEARS Buddha did everything that anybody could do. He went to all kinds of teachers, masters, scholars, wise men, sages, saints. And India is so full of these people that you need not seek or search; you simply move anywhere and you meet them. They are all over the place; if you don't seek them, they will seek you! And particularly in Buddha's time it was at a peak. The country was agog with only one thing: how to find something that transcends death.

But after six years' tremendous effort—austerities, fasting, and yoga postures—nothing had happened. Then one day... Even Buddhists have not been able to understand the significance of this story. This is the most important story in Gautam Buddha's life. Nothing else is comparable to it.

Just think of Gautam Buddha. He was his original self—that is his beauty and that is his greatness. He was not a Buddhist; he was simply himself. He had tried for six years continuously with different masters to find the truth, but nothing happened except frustration and failure. He was in great despair because he had been with all the great teachers that were available. Those

teachers themselves had to say to him—because of his sincerity, his honesty—"Whatever we knew we have taught to you. If you want more, then you will have to find it for yourself. This is all that we know. And we understand perfectly that you are not satisfied; neither are we satisfied, but we are not so courageous to go on trying to find. Even if it takes lives, go on trying to find it."

Finally, Buddha had to drop all the teachers and all the masters and start on his own. He worked tremendously hard. One of the most significant things happened that has to be remembered by all seekers, wherever they are in the world; it will always remain a significant milestone for future humanity.

One day he was staying by the side of Niranjana River. I have been to the place. The river is a small river; perhaps in the rainy season it becomes bigger, but when I went there in summer, it was just a small current of water.

He went down into the river to take a bath, but he had been fasting too long. He was so weak, and the current was so fast and strong that he was almost swept down the river. Somehow he caught hold of the roots of a tree, and in that moment an idea came to him: "I have become so weak by fasting because all the teachers, all the scriptures, constantly insist that unless you purify yourself by fasting, you cannot attain

enlightenment. I have weakened myself so much, but enlightenment has not happened. I cannot even get out of this small Niranjana River. How am I supposed to get out of the ocean of the whole world?"

In the Indian mythologies the world is compared to the ocean—*bhavsagar*. "How am I going to cross *bhavsagar*, the ocean of the world, if I cannot even cross the Niranjana River?"

It was a great moment of insight: "I have been unnecessarily torturing my body. It was not purification, it was weakening myself. It has not made me spiritual; it has made me sick."

Meantime, a woman in the town had made a promise to the tree under which Gautam Buddha was staying. Her promise was that if her son got well from a sickness, then she would come on the full-moon night and bring a bowl of sweets in gratitude to the deity of the tree.

It was a full-moon night, and just by coincidence Buddha was sitting under the tree. The woman thought, "My God, the deity himself is sitting under the tree waiting for me!" She was overjoyed. She placed the sweets at his feet, and she said, "I have never heard of the deity himself coming out of the tree and accepting the offering of us poor people, but you are great and you have helped me tremendously. Please forgive me for giving you so much trouble, but accept this small offering."

Buddha ate for the first time in years without any guilt.

All the religions have created guilt about everything. If you are eating something good—

guilty. If you are wearing something beautiful—guilty. If you are happy, something must be wrong. You should be serious, you should be sad—only then can you be thought to be religious. A religious person is not supposed to laugh.

Buddha, for the first time, was out of the grip of tradition. Nobody has analyzed the state of his mind in that moment, which is significant to the psychology of spiritual enlightenment. Buddha dropped out of the whole tradition, orthodoxy, all that he had been told, all that he had been conditioned for. He simply dropped everything.

He did not even ask the woman, "To what caste do you belong?" As far as I understand she must have belonged to the *Sudras*. It is written nowhere, but my conclusion has some reason because her name was Sujata. *Sujata* means "born into a high-caste family." Only somebody who is *not* born into a high-caste family can have such a name. One who is born in a high-caste family need not have such a name. You can find the poorest man in the town, and his name will be Dhanidas, "the rich man"... the ugliest woman in the town, and her name will be Sunderbai, "beautiful woman." People substitute names to add height to their reality. The name of the girl was Sujata.

Buddha dropped the structure that had surrounded him that evening. He did not ask the caste, the creed. He accepted the offering, he ate the sweets, and after many days he slept for the first time without any guilt about sleeping. Your so-called spiritual people are afraid of sleep. Even sleep is a sin—it has to be cut. The less you sleep, the greater a spiritual person you are.

That night Buddha slept just like a child, with no conception of what is right and what is wrong: innocent, unburdened from conditioning, tradition, orthodoxy, religion. He was not even worried that night about truth or enlightenment. He slept a deep, dreamless sleep, because dreams come to you only when you have desires. That night was absolutely desireless. He had no desire; hence, there was no question of any dream. In the morning when he opened his eyes, he was utterly silent. Outside it was absolutely silent. Soon the sun started to rise, and as the sun was rising, something inside him also started rising.

He was not searching for it; he was not looking for it. For the first time he was not desiring it and it happened—he was full of light.

The man Siddhartha became Gautam Buddha.

In that illumination, in that moment of enlightenment, *nirvana*, he did not find any God. The whole of existence is divine; there is no separate creator. The whole of existence is full of light and full of consciousness; hence, there is no God, but there is godliness.

It is a revolution in the world of religions. Buddha created a religion without God. For the first time God was no longer at the center of a religion. The human being becomes the center of religion, his innermost being becomes godliness, for which you do not have to go anywhere, you simply have to stop going outside. You have to remain within, slowly, slowly settling at your center. The day you are settled at the center, the explosion happens.

THE SMALLEST GESTURE

One day Buddha was walking with a disciple—it must have been just before he was enlightened. He had gathered a few disciples even before he became enlightened, because a light had started spreading—just like early in the morning, when the sun has not yet risen but the sky becomes red and the earth becomes full of light; the sun is just about to rise above the horizon. Before Buddha became enlightened, he had five disciples. He was walking with those five disciples; a fly sat on his head. He was talking to the disciples and without paying much attention, mechanically, he moved his hand and the fly went away. Then he stopped, closed his eyes. The disciples could not understand what was happening, but they all became silent—something precious was happening.

His face became luminous, and he raised his hand slowly, and again moved it near his forehead as if the fly were still sitting there—it was not there anymore. The disciples asked, "What are you doing? The fly is no longer there."

He said, "But now I am moving my hand consciously—that time I did it unconsciously. I missed an opportunity of being conscious. I was too much engaged in talking with you and the hand simply moved mechanically. It should have moved consciously. Now I am moving it as it should have moved."

This is what Buddha means when he talks about the path of virtue: to become so alert that even small acts, even small gestures, movements, all become full of awareness.

the life of
buddha

Buddha, Mahavira, Jesus... they are not part of the history

books. For them we need a totally different approach.

They are not part of history; they come from the beyond.

in search of enlightenment

The day before Gautam Buddha left the palace in the middle of the night, a child had been born to his wife. It is such a human story, so beautiful... Before leaving the palace, he wanted to see at least once the face of the child, his child, the symbol of his love with his wife. So he went into his wife's bedchamber. She was asleep, and the child was lying next to her, covered by a blanket. He wanted to remove the blanket and to see the face of the child, because perhaps he would never come back again.

H E WAS GOING ON AN unknown pilgrimage. Nothing could be known of what would happen in his life. He risked everything—his kingdom, his wife, his child, himself—in search of enlightenment, something he had only heard of as a possibility, something that had happened before to a few people who looked for it.

He was as full of doubts as anyone, but the moment of decision had come.... That very day he had seen death, he had seen old age, he had seen sickness, and he had also seen a sannyasin for the first time. It had become an ultimate question in him: "If there is death, then wasting time in the palace is dangerous. Before death comes I have to find something that is beyond death." He was determined to leave. But the human mind, human nature... He wanted to see the child's face—he had not even seen the face of his own child. But he was afraid that if he removed the blanket, if Yashodhara, his wife, woke up—there was every possibility she would wake up—she would ask, "What are you doing in the middle of the night in my room? And you seem to be ready to go somewhere..."

The chariot was standing outside the gate, everything was ready; he was just about to leave, and he had said to his charioteer, "Just wait a minute. Let me go and see the child's face. I may never come back again."

But he could not look because of the fear that Yashodhara might wake up, start crying, weeping, "Where are you going? What are you doing? What is this renunciation? What is this enlightenment?" One never knew—she might wake up the whole palace! The old father would come, and the whole thing would be spoiled. So he simply escaped.

After twelve years, when he was enlightened, the first thing he wanted to do was to come back to his palace to apologize to his father, to his wife, to his son who must be now twelve years of age. He was aware that they would be angry. The father was very angry—he was the first one

to meet him, and for half an hour he continued abusing Buddha. But then suddenly the father became aware that he was saying so many things and his son was just standing there like a marble statue, as if nothing was affecting him.

The father looked at him, and Gautam Buddha said, "That's what I wanted. Please dry your tears. Look at me: I am not the same boy who left the palace. Your son died long ago. I look similar to your son, but my whole consciousness is different. You just look."

The father said, "I am seeing it. For half an hour I have been abusing you, and that is enough proof that you have changed. Otherwise know how temperamental you were; you could not stand so silently. What has happened to you?"

Buddha said, "I will tell you. Just let me first see my wife and my child. They must be waiting—they must have heard that I have come."

The first thing his wife said to him was, "I can see that you are transformed. These twelve years were a great suffering, but not because you had gone; I suffered because you did not tell me. If you had simply told me that you were

going to seek the truth, do you think I would have prevented you? You have insulted me very badly. This is the wound that I have been carrying for twelve years.

'It was not that you had gone in search of truth—that is something to rejoice in. Not that you had gone to become enlightened—I would not have prevented you. Like you, I also belong to the warrior caste; do you think I am so weak that I would have cried and screamed and stopped you?

"All these twelve years my only suffering was that you did not trust me. I would have allowed you, I would have given you a send-off, I would have come up to the chariot to say goodbye. So first I want to ask the only question that has been in my mind for these twelve years, which is that whatever you have attained… and it certainly seems you have attained something. You are no longer the same person who left this palace; you radiate a different light, your presence is totally new and fresh, your eyes are as pure and clear as a cloudless sky. You have become so beautiful… you were always beautiful, but this beauty seems to be not of this world. Some grace from the beyond has descended on you. My question is:

Whatever you have attained, was it not possible to attain it here in this palace? Can the palace prevent the truth?"

It was a tremendously intelligent question, and Gautam Buddha had to agree: "I could have attained it here, but I had no idea at that moment. Now I can say that I could have attained it here in this palace; there was no need to go to the mountains, there was no need to go anywhere. I had to go inside, and that could have happened anywhere. This palace was as good as any other place, but only now I can say it. At that moment I had no idea.

"So you have to forgive me, because it is not that I did not trust you or your courage. In fact, I was doubtful of myself. If I had seen you wake up, and if I had seen the child, I may have started wondering, 'What am I doing, leaving my beautiful wife, whose total love, whose total devotion is for me. And leaving my day-old child... if I am to leave him then why did you give birth to him? I am escaping from my responsibilities.' If my old father had awakened, it would have become impossible for me.

"It was not that I did not trust you; it was that I did not trust myself. I knew that there was a wavering; I was not total in renouncing. A part of me was saying, 'What are you doing?' and a part of me was saying, 'This is the time to do it. If you don't do it now it will become more and more difficult. Your father is preparing to crown you. Once you are crowned as king, it will be more difficult.'"

Yashodhara said to him, "This is the only question that I wanted to ask, and I am immensely happy that you have been absolutely truthful in saying that it can be attained here, that it can be attained anywhere. Now your son, who is standing there, a little boy of twelve years, has been continually asking about you, and I have been telling him, 'Just wait. He will come back; he cannot be so cruel, he cannot be so unkind, he cannot be so inhuman. One day he will come. Perhaps whatever he has gone to realize is taking time; once he has realized it, the first thing he will do is to come back.'

"So your son is here, and I want you to tell me, what heritage are you leaving for him?

What have you got to give to your son? You have given him life—now what else?"

Buddha had nothing except his begging bowl, so he called his son, whose name was Rahul, the name Gautam Buddha had given him. He called Rahul close to him and gave him the begging bowl. He said, "I don't have anything. This is my only possession; from now onward I will have to use my hands as a begging bowl to take my food, to beg my food. By giving you this begging bowl, I am initiating you into *sannyas*. That is the only treasure that I have found, and I would like you to find it too."

He said to Yashodhara, "You have to be ready to become a part of my commune of sannyasins," and he initiated his wife. The old man had come and was watching the whole scene. He said to Gautam Buddha, "Why are you leaving me out? Don't you want to share what you have found with your old father? My death is very close... initiate me also."

Buddha said, "I had come, in fact, to take you all with me, because what I have found is a far greater kingdom—a kingdom that is going to last forever, a kingdom that cannot be conquered. I came here so that you could feel my presence, so that you could feel my realization and I could persuade you to become my fellow-travelers." So he initiated all three of them.

He had given his son the name Rahul from the Indian mythology about a moon eclipse. In the mythology, the moon is a person, a god, and he has two enemies: one is Rahu and the other is Ketu. When the moon eclipse happens, it happens because Rahu and Ketu catch hold of the moon. They try to kill it, but each time the moon escapes from their grip.

> *If you are courageous enough to risk everything for being alert and aware, enlightenment is going to happen*

Gautam Buddha had given the name Rahul to his son because he thought, "This son of mine is going to be my greatest hindrance; he is going to be my greatest enemy. He will prevent me from going to the Himalayas. Love for him, attachment to him, will be my chains." That's why he had given him the name Rahul.

They all moved into the forest outside the city where all of Buddha's disciples were staying. In the first sermon to the disciples that evening he told them, "My wife Yashodhara has asked me a question that is of tremendous importance. She has asked me, 'Was it not possible to become enlightened in the palace as a king?' And I have told her the truth: There is no question of any place, any time. One can become enlightened anywhere, but at that time nobody was there to say it to me. I had no idea of where it was to be found, whom I had to ask, where I had to go. I just jumped into the unknown. But now I can say that wherever you are, if you are courageous enough to risk everything for being alert and aware, enlightenment is going to happen."

sermons in silence

THERE IS NO language that can express the experience of enlightenment. There cannot be, by the very nature of the phenomenon. Enlightenment happens beyond mind, and language is part of the mind. Enlightenment is experienced in utter silence.

If you want to call silence a language, then of course enlightenment has a language— which consists of silence, which consists of blissfulness, which consists of ecstasy, which consists of innocence. But this is not the ordinary meaning of language. The ordinary meaning is that words have to be used as a vehicle to convey something. Silence cannot be conveyed by words; nor can ecstasy nor love nor blissfulness. In fact, enlightenment can be seen, can be understood, can be felt—but cannot be heard and cannot be spoken.

When Gautam Buddha became enlightened, he remained silent for seven days. All of existence waited breathlessly to hear him, to hear his music, to hear his soundless song, his words coming from the land of the beyond— words of truth. All of existence was waiting and those seven days seemed like seven centuries.

The story is tremendously beautiful. Up to a certain point it is factual and beyond that it becomes mythological, but by mythological I do not mean it becomes a lie. There are a few truths that can be expressed only through myths. He

attained enlightenment—that is a truth. He remained silent for seven days—that is a truth. That the whole of existence waited to hear him is a truth—but only for those who had experienced something of enlightenment and who had experienced the waiting existence, not for everybody.

But still it can be understood that existence rejoices whenever somebody becomes enlightened because it is a part of existence itself that is coming to its highest expression, a part of existence that is becoming an Everest, the highest peak. Naturally, it is existence's crowning glory. It is the very longing of the whole to one day become enlightened, one day to dispel all unconsciousness and flood the whole of existence with consciousness and light, to destroy all misery and bring as many flowers of joy as possible.

Beyond this point it becomes pure mythology, but still it has its own significance and its own truth.

The gods in heaven became worried. One thing has to be understood: Buddhism does not believe in a God, nor does Jainism believe in a God, but they believe in *gods*. They are far more democratic in their concepts than Mohammedanism, Judaism, or Christianity. Those religions are more elitist. One God, one religion, one holy scripture, one prophet—they are very monopolistic. But Buddhism has a

different approach, far more democratic, far more human. It conceives millions of gods.

In fact, every being in existence has to become a god one day. When he becomes enlightened, he will be a god. According to Buddhism there is no God as a creator, and that brings dignity to every being. You are not puppets, you have an individuality and a freedom and a pride. Nobody can create you, nobody can destroy you. Hence, another concept has come out of this: Nobody can save you except yourself. In Christianity there is the idea of the savior; in Judaism there is the idea of the savior. If there is a God, he can send his messengers, prophets, messiahs to save you. Even liberating yourself is not within your hands. Even your liberation is going to be a sort of slavery—somebody else liberates you, and a liberation that is in somebody else's hands is not much of a liberation.

Freedom has to be achieved, not to be begged for. Freedom has to be snatched, not to be prayed for. A freedom that is given to you as a gift out of compassion is not of much value. Hence, in Buddhism there is no savior either. But there are gods—those who have become enlightened before. Since eternity, millions of people must have become enlightened; they are all gods.

These gods became disturbed when seven days of silence passed after Gautam Buddha's enlightenment, because it rarely happens that a human being becomes enlightened. It is such a rare and unique phenomenon that the very soul of existence waits for it, longs for it. Thousands of years pass, and then somebody becomes enlightened. What if Gautam Buddha is not going to speak, what if he chooses to remain silent? This is a natural possibility because silence is the only right language for enlightenment. The moment you try to bring it into language it becomes distorted. And the distortion happens on many levels.

First, it becomes distorted when you drag it down from its height, from the peaks to the dark valleys of the mind. The first distortion happens there. Almost ninety percent of its reality is lost.

Then you speak. The second distortion happens because what you can conceive in the deepest core of your heart is one thing; the moment you bring it into expression as words, that is another thing. You feel great love, but when you say to someone, "I love you," suddenly you realize the word *love* is too small to express what you are feeling. It seems embarrassing to use it.

The third distortion happens when it is heard by somebody else, because he has his own ideas, his own conditionings, his own thoughts, opinions, philosophies, ideologies, prejudices. He will immediately interpret it according to himself. By the time it reaches the person, it is no longer the same thing that had started from the highest peak of your consciousness. It has gone through so many changes that it is altogether something else. So it has happened many times that enlightened people have not spoken. Out of a hundred enlightened people, perhaps one may have chosen to speak.

Gautam Buddha was such a rare human being, so cultured, so articulate that if he had chosen to remain silent the world would have missed a great opportunity.

The gods came down, touched the feet of Gautam Buddha and asked him to speak: "Existence is waiting. The trees are waiting, the mountains are waiting, the valleys are waiting. The clouds are waiting, the stars are waiting. Don't frustrate everyone. Don't be so unkind, have some mercy and speak."

But Gautam Buddha had his own argument. He said, "I can understand your compassion, and I would like to speak. For seven days I have been wavering between the two, whether to speak or not to speak, and every argument goes for not speaking. I have not been able to find a single argument in favor of speaking. I am going to be misunderstood, so what is the point when you are going to be misunderstood—which is absolutely certain. I am going to be condemned; nobody is going to listen to me in the way that the words of an enlightened man have to be listened to. Listening needs a certain training, a discipline; it is not just hearing.

"And even if somebody understands me, he is not going to take a single step, because every step is dangerous; it is walking on a razor's edge. I am not against speaking, I just cannot see that there is any use, and I have found every argument against it."

The gods looked at each other. What Gautam Buddha was saying was right. They went aside to discuss what to do next. "We cannot say that what he is saying is wrong, but still we would like him to speak. Some way has to be found to convince him." They discussed for a long time and finally they came to a conclusion.

They came back to Gautam Buddha and they said, "We have found one single, small argument. It is very small in comparison to all the arguments that go against it, but still we would like you to consider. Our argument is that you may be misunderstood by ninety-nine percent of the people, but you cannot say that you will be misunderstood by a hundred percent of the people. You have to give at least a little margin—just one percent. That one percent is not small in this vast universe; that one percent is a big enough portion. Perhaps out of that one percent, few will be able to follow the path.

"But even if one person in the whole universe becomes enlightened because of your speaking, it is worth it. Enlightenment is such a great experience that even if your whole life's effort can make one person enlightened you have done well. To ask for more is not right; this is more than enough. There are a few people— you must be aware, as we are aware—who are

just on the borderline. A little push, a little encouragement, a little hope and perhaps they will cross the boundary of ignorance, they will cross the boundary of bondage, they will come out of their prisons. You have to speak."

Gautam Buddha closed his eyes and he thought for a few moments, and he said, "I cannot deny that much possibility. It is not much, but I do understand that all my arguments, howsoever great, are small in comparison to the compassion. I will live for at least forty-two years, and if I can make a single individual enlightened I will feel immensely rewarded. I will speak. You can go back unburdened of your worry and concern."

He spoke for forty-two years, and certainly not just one, but about two dozen people became enlightened. These two dozen people were the people who learned the art of listening, who learned the art of being silent. They did not become enlightened because of what Buddha was saying, they became enlightened because they could feel what Buddha *was*—his presence, his vibe, his silence, his depth, his height.

These two dozen people were not becoming enlightened just by listening to the words of Gautam Buddha. The words helped—they helped them to be in the presence of Gautam Buddha, they helped them to understand the beauty that ordinary words take on when they are used by an enlightened person.

Ordinary gestures become so graceful, ordinary eyes become so beautiful, with such depth and meaning. The way Buddha walks has a different quality to it; the way he sleeps has a different significance to it. These were the people who tried to understand not what Gautam Buddha was *saying*, but what he was *being*. His being is the only authentic language.

Millions heard him and became knowledgeable. The day he died, the same day, thirty-two schools sprang up, thirty-two divisions amongst the disciples, because they differed in their interpretations of what Gautam Buddha had said. Every effort was made that they should gather together and compile whatever they had heard from Gautam Buddha, but all their efforts were failures. There are thirty-two versions, so different that one cannot believe how people can hear one person in so many ways.

Even today those thirty-two schools go on quarreling. For twenty-five centuries they have not been reconciled with each other. In fact, they have gone farther and farther away from each other. Now they have become independent philosophies, each proposing that "This is what Gautam Buddha has said and everybody else is wrong. This is the holy scripture; others are just collections by people who don't understand."

It is one of the great puzzles: What is the language of enlightenment? The *being* of the enlightened person is his language. To be in contact with him, to drop all defenses, to open all the doors of your heart, to allow his love to reach to you, to allow his vibe to become your vibe…. Slowly, slowly, if one is ready, unafraid, then something transpires which nobody can see. Something has happened; something that has not been said has been heard. Something that is not possible to bring into words has been conveyed through silence.

Buddha was speaking against Brahmans, against Hindus, but all his great disciples were Brahmans. It seems sensible because he was appealing to the best in the society. Although he was against Brahmans, the Brahmans were at the top of the ladder and out of the Brahmans came the greater part of the intelligentsia.

Sariputta was a Brahman, Moggalayan was a Brahman, Mahakashyapa was a Brahman.

They all had come to Buddha not because they were illiterate idiots, the rejected—gamblers, prostitutes, tax collectors, thieves—no, but because they were great scholars and they could understand that what Buddha was saying was right.

When Sariputta came to Buddha, he himself had five hundred disciples of his own coming with him—all great scholars. He had come first to have a discussion, and Buddha was very happy: what could be more welcome? But Buddha asked, "Have you experienced the truth, or are you only a great scholar? I have heard your name…."

Looking at Buddha for a moment in silence, as if looking in a mirror, utterly naked, Sariputta said "I am a great scholar, but as far as knowing the truth is concerned, I have not known it."

Buddha said, "Then it will be very difficult to argue. Argument is possible between two people who don't know truth. They can argue till eternity because neither knows. Both are ignorant, so they can go on playing with words and logic and quotations and scriptures. But because neither knows, there is no possibility of their coming to a conclusion. At the most what can happen is that whoever is more clever and cunning and tricky may defeat the other, and the other will become the follower of the more cunning or more sophisticated. But is this any decision about truth?

'Or there is a possibility of a meeting of two people who both have realized the truth, but then there is no way to argue. What is there to argue about? They will sit silently; perhaps they may smile, or hold each other's hands, but what is there to say? Looking into each other's eyes

they will see that there is nothing to say—we both know the same things, we are in the same space—so there will be only silence.

"The third possibility is that one knows and one does not know. Then it is going to be very troublesome because the one who knows cannot translate what he knows into the language of the ignorant one. And the one who does not know will be unnecessarily wasting his time, his mind, because he cannot convince the one who knows. The whole world cannot convince the person who knows, because he knows and you don't know. You may be all together...."

Buddha said, "You have come with your five hundred disciples. You don't know, and it is absolutely certain that among these five hundred disciples no one knows; otherwise he would not be your disciple, he would be your master. You are more scholarly, they are less scholarly. You are older, they are younger. They are your disciples. But how are we going to discuss anything? I am ready... but I *know*. One thing is certain, you cannot convert me. The only possibility is that you will be converted, so think twice."

But Sariputta was already converted and he was intelligent enough; he had defeated many

great scholars. It was a tradition in India in those days that scholars would move all over the country defeating other scholars.

Unless a person had defeated all the scholars, he would not be recognized by the scholarly mob as a wise man. But to stand before a buddha, before one who knows, it is not a question of your scholarship and how many scholars you have defeated.

Buddha said, "I am ready. If you want to argue I am ready, but what argument is possible? I have eyes; you don't have eyes. I cannot explain to you what light is. You cannot have any idea what light is. You will hear only the word *light* but the word will not have any meaning for you. It will be without content—heard, but not understood.

"So if you are really interested in truth, and not in getting defeated or being victorious... because that is not my interest. I have arrived. Who cares to defeat anybody? For what? If you are interested in truth then be here and do what I say. You can argue later on when you have come to know something substantial, existential. Then you can argue."

But Sariputta was a tremendously intelligent man. He said, "I know that neither can I argue

now, nor will I be able to argue then. You have finished my argumentation. Now I cannot argue because I don't have eyes; then I will not be able to argue because I will have eyes. But I am going to stay."

He stayed with his five hundred disciples. He said to the disciples, "Now I am no longer your master. Here is the man; I will be sitting by his side as his disciple. Please forget me as your master. If you want to be here, he is your master now."

One day a man came up to Gautam Buddha in the morning, and asked him, "Does God exist?" Buddha looked at the man for a moment, and then he said, "Yes." The man could not believe it because he had heard that Buddha does not believe in God. Now, what to make of his answer?

One of Buddha's closest disciples, Ananda, was with him. He was shocked. Buddha had never said with such certainty, without any ifs and buts, a simple yes—to God! He had his whole life been fighting against the idea of God.

But there was an agreement between Buddha and Ananda. Ananda was Buddha's elder cousin. When he was ready to become a disciple of Buddha, Ananda had asked beforehand, "You have to promise me a few things. Right now I am your elder cousin. After the initiation I will be your disciple; then whatever you say I will have to do. But right now I can ask you for something and you will have to do it."

Buddha said, "I know you. You cannot ask anything that will put your younger cousin in any difficulty. You can ask."

Ananda said, "They are not big things, just simple things. One is that every night before going to sleep, if I want to ask something, you will have to answer. You can't say, 'I am tired from the day's journey, and so many people and so many meetings...' You will have to answer me. I will never ask in the day, I will not disturb you the whole day. But I am a human being and I am not enlightened; certain questions may arise."

Buddha said, "That is accepted."

In the same way Ananda asked two more things: "One is that you will never tell me to go anywhere else; I will always be with you, to serve you till my last breath. You will not tell me, 'Now you go and spread my message,' the way you send others. You cannot send me."

Buddha said, "Okay, that's not a problem."

And third, Ananda said, "If I ask you to give some time to somebody, at any hour—it may be an odd hour, in the middle of the night—you will have to meet the person. That much privilege you have to give me."

Buddha said, "That, too, is okay because I know you. You will not take advantage of these conditions...."

Ananda was puzzled by Buddha's answer that God exists. But as he could not ask in the day, he had to wait for the night. In the afternoon, another man came and asked the same question: "Is there a God?" And Buddha said, "No, not at all."

Now, things became more complicated! Ananda was almost in a state of falling apart. But

> *Belief as such is the barrier; it does not matter what belief it is, true or false*

this was nothing. In the evening, a third man came, and he sat in front of Buddha and asked, "Will you say something about God?"

Buddha looked at him, closed his eyes, and remained silent. The man also closed his eyes. They sat in silence for half an hour; then the man touched Buddha's feet and said, "Thank you for your answer," and went away.

Now, it was too much. The time was passing so slowly and Ananda was boiling within; when everybody was gone, he jumped up. He said, "This is too much! You should take care, at least, of us poor disciples. Those three persons don't know all the three answers, they only know one answer. But we are with you, we have heard all the answers. You should think of us too, we have been going crazy. If this is going to continue, what will happen to us?"

Buddha said, "You should remember one thing. First, those questions were not your questions; those answers were not given to you. Why should you jump into it? It is none of your business. It was something between me and those three people."

Ananda said, "That I can understand. It is not my question, and you have not answered me.

But I have ears and I can hear; I heard the question, I heard the answer. And all three answers are contradiction upon contradiction. First you say yes, then you say no, and then you remain silent, you don't say anything and that man touched your feet and said, 'Thank you for your answer.' And we are sitting here… there has been no answer at all!"

Buddha said, "You think about life in terms of absolutes; that's your trouble. Life is relative. To the first man, the answer was yes; it was relative to him, related to the implications of his questions, his being, his life. That man to whom I said yes was an atheist; he does not believe in God and I do not want to support his stupid atheism. He goes on proclaiming there is no God. Even if a small space is left unexplored, perhaps in that space God exists. You can say with absolute certainty that there is no God when you have explored all of existence. That is possible only at the very end, and that man was simply believing that there was no God—he had no existential experience of there being no God. I had to shatter him, I had to bring him down to earth. I had to hit him hard on the head. My yes was relative to that person, to his whole personality. His question was not just words. The same question from somebody else may have received another answer.

"And that's what happened when I said to the other person, 'No.' The question was the same, the words were the same, but the man behind those words was different, so the relationship between the words and the implications had changed. It is relative. The second man was as much an idiot as was the first, but on the opposite pole. He believed there is a God, and he had come to get my support for his belief. I don't support anybody's belief because belief as such is the barrier. It does not matter what belief it is, true or false. No belief is true, no belief is false; all beliefs are simply idiotic. I had to say to that man, 'No.'

"The third man had come with no belief. He had not asked me, 'Is there a God?' No, he had come with an open heart, with no mind, no belief, no ideology. He was a sane man, intelligent. He asked me, 'Would you say something about God?' He was not in search of somebody's support for his belief system, he was not in search of a faith, he was not asking with a prejudiced mind. He was asking about my experience: 'Would you say something about God?'

"I could see that this man has no belief, this way or that; he is innocent. With such an innocent person, language is meaningless. I cannot say yes, I cannot say no; only silence is the answer. So I closed my eyes and remained silent. And my feeling about the man proved to be true. He closed his eyes—seeing me close my eyes, he closed his eyes. He understood my answer: Be silent, go in. He remained in silence for half an hour with me and received the answer that God is not a theory, a belief you have to be for or against. That's why he thanked me for the answer.

"And you are puzzled about what answer he thanked me for? He received the answer that silence is divine, and to be silent is to be godly; there is no other god than silence. And he went tremendously fulfilled, contented. He has found the answer. I have not given him the answer; *he* has found the answer. I simply allowed him to have a taste of my presence."

the peaceful warrior

GAUTAM BUDDHA was surrounded by a crowd that was abusing him, using ugly words, obscene words, because he was against the organized religion of the Hindus and against the Hindu holy scriptures, the *Vedas*. He had condemned the priesthood, saying that these were exploiters, parasites. Naturally, the Brahmans were enraged.

This was a Brahman village through which he was passing and the Brahmans surrounded him and said every kind of bad thing that they could manage. He listened silently. His disciples became angry, but because Buddha was present it was not courteous to say anything. The master was standing so silent, and listening as if these people were saying sweet things.

Finally Buddha said to them, "If the things that you wanted to say to me are finished,

> *...you cannot make me angry unless I accept your humiliation, your insult*

I would like to go on to the next village where people are waiting for me. But if you are not finished, after a few days I will be returning and I will inform you. Then I will have enough time to listen to all that you want to say."

One man said, "Do you think that we are saying something? We are condemning you! Do you understand or not? Because anybody else would become angry, and you are standing silently...."

The statement that Buddha made to these village people is immensely significant. He said, "You have come a little too late. If you had come ten years ago when I was as insane as you are, not a single person would have left here alive."

Ten years ago he was a prince, a warrior, one of the best archers of his time, a great swordsman, and those Brahmans...he could have removed their heads with a single blow, without any difficulty, because those Brahmans know nothing about swords or arrows or being a warrior. He would have cut them almost like vegetables.

He said, "You have come late. Ten years ago if you had come...but now I am no longer insane; I cannot react. But I would like to ask you one question. In the last village people came with sweets and fruits and flowers to receive me; however, we take food only once a day and we had already taken our food. And we don't carry things. So we had to tell them, 'You please forgive us, we cannot accept sweets, flowers. We accept your love, but these things you will have to keep.' I want to ask you," he said to this angry crowd, "what must they have done with the sweets and flowers they had brought as presents for us?"

One man said, "What is the mystery in it? They must have distributed the sweets in the village."

Buddha said, "That makes me very sad. What will you do?—because I don't accept what you have brought, in the same way I did not accept the sweets and the flowers and other things that the people brought to me in the other village. If I don't accept your obscenity, your ugly words, your dirty words—if I don't accept them, what can you do? What are you going to do with all this garbage that you have come with? You will have to take it back to your homes and give it to your wives, to your children, to your neighbors. You will have to distribute it because I refuse to take it. And you cannot make me angry unless I accept your humiliation, your insult.

"Ten years ago I was not conscious; if somebody had insulted me he would have lost his life immediately. I had no idea that insulting me is his problem, and that I have nothing to do with it. I can simply listen and go on my way."

There was one man who was a mad murderer. He had taken a vow that he would kill one thousand people, not fewer than that, because

the society had not treated him well. He would take his revenge by killing one thousand people. And from every person killed he would take one finger and make a rosary around his neck—one thousand fingers. Because of this, his name became Angulimala, the man with a rosary of fingers.

He killed nine hundred and ninety-nine people. Nobody would move in those parts; wherever people came to know that Angulimala

STILLNESS

Buddha always slept in the same posture. He would remain the whole night in the same posture; he would not change his position at all. That posture has become famous—there are many statues with Buddha in that posture in Ceylon, China, Japan, and India. If you go to Ajanta, there is a statue of Buddha lying down. That posture was reported by his disciple Ananda: Buddha slept in the same posture the whole night, never even changing sides.

One day Ananda asked, "One thing puzzles me. You remain in the same posture the whole night. Are you asleep or not? If someone is asleep, he will change his posture. Even while you are asleep—or appear to be asleep—it looks as if you are alert. It seems you know what the body is doing; you will not even change your posture unconsciously."

Buddha said, "Yes, when the mind is silent, not dreaming, only the body sleeps. The consciousness remains alert."

was, the traffic would stop. And then it became very difficult for him to find one man, and only one more man was needed.

Buddha was moving toward a forest; people came to him from the villages and they said, "Don't go! Angulimala is there, that mad murderer! He doesn't think twice, he simply murders; and he will not think about the fact that you are a buddha. Don't go that way; there is another path, you can move on that one, but don't go through this forest!"

Buddha said, "If I don't go, then who will go? And he is waiting for one more, so I have to go."

Angulimala had almost completed his vow. And he was a man of energy because he was fighting the whole society. Only one man, and he had killed a thousand people. Kings were afraid of him, generals were afraid, and the government and the law and the police— nobody could do anything. But Buddha said, "He is a man, he needs me. I must take the risk. Either he will kill me or I will kill him."

This is what buddhas do: they stake their lives. Buddha went. Even the closest disciples who had said that they would remain with him up to the very end started lagging behind because this was dangerous! So when Buddha reached the hill where Angulimala was sitting on a rock, there was no one behind him, he was alone. All the disciples had disappeared Angulimala looked at this innocent man: childlike, so beautiful, he thought, that even a murderer felt compassion for him. He thought, "This man seems to be absolutely unaware that I am here, otherwise nobody goes along this path." And the man looked so innocent, so beautiful, that even Angulimala thought, 'It is

not good to kill this man. I'll leave him, I can find somebody else."

Then he said to Buddha, "Go back! Stop there now and go back! Don't move a step forward! I am Angulimala, and these are nine hundred and ninety-nine fingers here, and I need one finger more—even if my mother comes I will kill her and fulfill my vow! So don't come near, I'm dangerous! And I am not a believer in religion, I'm not bothered who you are. You may be a very good monk, a great saint maybe, but I don't care! I only care about the finger, and your finger is as good as anybody else's so don't come a single step further, otherwise I will kill you. Stop!" But Buddha continued moving.

Then Angulimala thought, "Either this man is deaf or mad!" He again shouted, "Stop! Don't move!"

Buddha said, "I stopped long ago; I am not moving, Angulimala, you are moving. I stopped long ago. All movement has stopped because all motivation has stopped. When there is no motivation, how can movement happen? There is no goal for me, I have achieved the goal, so why should I move? You are moving—and I say to you: you stop!"

Angulimala was sitting on the rock and he started laughing. He said, "You are really mad! I am sitting and you say to me that I am moving. And you are moving and you say that you have stopped. You are really a fool or mad—or I don't know what type, what manner of man you are!"

Buddha came near and he said, "I have heard that you need one more finger. As far as this body is concerned, my goal is achieved; this body is useless. When I die people will burn it, it

SEEDS OF SALVATION

A young child died; the father of the child had already died and the woman was living only for this child. That child was her whole life and her only hope; otherwise, there was nothing for her to live for. And the child died—she was almost on the verge of going crazy. She wouldn't allow anyone to take the child to the crematorium. She was hugging the child in the hope that perhaps he might start breathing again. She was ready to give her own life if the child could live.

The people said, "This is not possible, it is against the law of nature." But she was in such misery that she could not listen to anybody. Then somebody said, "The best way is, let us take this woman to Gautam Buddha who, just by chance, is in the village."

This appealed to the woman. A man like Gautam Buddha can do anything, and this is a small miracle—nothing much—to make the child start breathing again. She went, crying and weeping, put the child's dead body at the feet of Buddha, and said to him, "You are a great master, you know the secrets of life and death, and I have come with great hope. Make my child alive again."

Buddha said, "That I will do, but you have to fulfill a condition before I do it."

She said, "I am ready to fulfill any condition. I am ready to give my life, but let my child live."

Buddha said, "No, the condition you have to fulfill is very simple. You just go around the village and find a few mustard seeds from a house where death has never happened."

She was in such despair, she went from one house to another. And all those people said, "We can give you as many mustard seeds as you want, but those mustard seeds will not help you. Not only one, but many have died in our family; perhaps thousands have died over the generations."

By the evening, a great awakening had happened to the woman. She had gone through the whole village and got the same reply.... They were all ready to help her but they said, "These mustard seeds won't help. Buddha has made it clear to you, 'Bring the mustard seeds from a family where nobody has ever died.'"

By the evening, when she returned, she was a totally different woman. She was not the same woman who had come in the morning. She had become absolutely aware that death is a reality of life—it cannot be changed.

And what is the point? "Even if my child lives for a few years, he will have to die again. In the first place it is not possible; in the second place, even if it were possible, it is pointless."

Now there were no more tears in her eyes; she was very quiet, serene. A tremendous understanding had come to her: she had been asking for the impossible. She dropped that desire. She came and fell at Buddha's feet.

Buddha said, "Where are the mustard seeds? I have been waiting the whole day."

The woman, instead of crying, laughed. She said, "You played a good joke! Forget all about the child, what is gone is gone.

"Now I have come to be initiated and to become a *sannyasin*. The way you have found the truth that never dies, I also want

to find. I am no longer concerned with the child or anybody else. My concern is now, how to find the truth the never dies, the truth that is life itself."

Buddha said, "Forgive me that I had to ask you for something I knew was impossible. But it was a simple device to bring you to your senses, and it worked."

will be of no use to anyone. You can use it, your vow can be fulfilled: cut off my finger and cut off my head. I have come on purpose because this is the last chance for my body to be used in some way; otherwise people will burn it."

Angulimala said, "What are you saying? I thought that I was the only madman around here. And don't try to be clever because I am dangerous, I can still kill you!"

Buddha said, "Before you kill me, do one thing. Just the wish of a dying man—cut off a branch of this tree." Angulimala hit his sword against the tree and a big branch fell down. Buddha said, "Just one thing more: join it again to the tree!"

Angulimala said, "Now I know perfectly that you are mad—I can cut, but I cannot join."

Then Buddha started laughing and he said, "When you can only destroy and cannot create, you should not destroy. Destruction can be done by children; there is no bravery in it. This branch can be cut by a child, but to join it a master is needed. And if you cannot even join back a branch to the tree, how can you cut off human heads? Have you ever thought about it?"

Angulimala closed his eyes, fell down at Buddha's feet, and he said, "You lead me on that path!" And it is said that in a single moment he became enlightened.

Next day he was a *bhikkhu*, a beggar, Buddha's monk, and begging in the city. The whole city was closed up. People were so afraid, they said, "Even if he has become a beggar he cannot be believed. That man is so dangerous!" People were not out on the roads. When Angulimala came to beg, nobody was there to give him food, because who would take the risk? People were standing on their terraces looking down. And then they started throwing stones at him because he had killed nine hundred and ninety-nine men of that town. Almost every family had been a victim, so they started throwing stones.

Angulimala fell down on the street, blood was flowing from all over his body, he had many wounds. And Buddha came with his disciples and he said, "Look! Angulimala, how are you feeling?"

Angulimala opened his eyes and said, "I am so grateful to you. They can kill the body but they cannot touch me. And that is what I was doing my whole life and never realized the fact."

Buddha said, "Angulimala has become enlightened; he has become a Brahman, a knower of Brahma."

physician of the soul

GAUTAM BUDDHA came into a town. That town had a blind man who was a great logician, very rational, and the whole town had tried to tell him that light exists, but nobody could prove it.

There is no way to prove light. Either you can see it or you cannot see it, but there is no other proof.

The blind man said, "I am ready. I can touch things and I can feel them with my hands. You bring your light and I would like to touch it and feel it."

But light is not something tangible. They said, "No, it cannot be touched or felt."

He said, "I have other ways. I can smell it, I can taste it. I can beat on it and hear the sound. But these are my only instruments—my ears, my nose, my tongue, my hands—I am making available to you all my faculties. Should I listen to my own common sense, or should I listen to you? I say there is no light; it is simply an invention, an invention of cunning people to deceive simple people like me so that you can prove that I am blind and you have eyes. The whole strategy is that you are not interested in light, you are interested in proving that you have eyes and I don't have eyes. You want to be higher, superior. Because you cannot be logically, rationally superior to me you have brought in something absurd. Forget all about it, you are all blind. Nobody has seen light because light does not exist."

When they heard that Buddha had come to the town, the people said, "It is a good opportunity. We should take our logician the blind man to Gautam Buddha; perhaps he can convince him—we cannot find a better man to do it."

They brought the blind man to Gautam Buddha. They told the story that was going on. One blind man was proving them all blind, was proving that there is no light, and they were absolutely incapable of proving the existence of light.

The words of Gautam Buddha are worth remembering. He said, "You have brought him to the wrong person. He does not need a philosopher, he needs a physician. It is not a question of convincing him, it is a question of curing his eyes. But don't be worried, I have my

> " The bee never gathers for tomorrow; today is enough unto itself "

LIKE A HONEYBEE

The *bhikkhu*, the Buddhist sannyasin, goes from house to house; he never asks from just one house because that may be too much of a burden. So he asks from many houses—just a little bit from one house, a little bit from another so he is not a burden on anybody. And he never goes to the same house again. This is called madhukari—like a honeybee. The bee goes from one flower to another, and goes on moving from flower to flower—it is nonpossessive. It takes so little from one flower that the beauty is not marred, the perfume is not destroyed. The flower never becomes aware of the bee; it comes so silently and goes so silently.

Buddha says: The man of awareness lives in this world like a bee. He never mars the beauty of this world, he never destroys the perfume of this world. He lives silently, moves silently. He asks only as much as is needed. His life is simple, it is not complex. He does not gather for tomorrow. The bee never gathers for tomorrow; today is enough unto itself.

PORTRAIT

For five hundred years after Buddha's death his statue was not created, his picture was not painted. For five hundred years, whenever a Buddhist temple was created, only the picture of the bodhi tree was there. That was beautiful—because in that moment when Gautam Siddhartha became Buddha, he was not there, only the tree was there. He had disappeared for a moment and only the tree remained.

personal physician with me." One of the emperors of those days had given his own personal physician to Gautam Buddha to take care of him twenty-four hours a day, to be with him like a shadow.

He said to the physician, "You take care of this man's eyes."

The physician looked at the man's eyes and he said, "It is not a difficult case; a certain disease is crippling his eyes, which can be cured. It may take at the most six months."

Buddha left his physician in the village, and after six months the man opened his eyes. All his logic, all his rationality disappeared. He said, "My God, I was telling those people that they were cheating me, deceiving me. Light exists— I was blind! Had I accepted the idea of my blindness before, there would have been no need for me to live my whole life in blindness."

Buddha had gone far away in those six months, but the man came dancing, fell at

Buddha's feet and said to him, "Your compassion is great that you did not argue with me, that you did not try to convince me about the light, but gave me a physician."

Buddha said, "This is my work. There are spiritually blind people all around. My work is not to convince them about the beauty, the blissfulness, the ecstasy of existence; my work is that of a physician."

One morning a great king, Prasenjita, came to Gautam Buddha. He had in one of his hands a beautiful lotus flower, and in the other hand a most precious diamond. He had come because his wife was persistent: "When Gautam Buddha is here, you waste your time with idiots, talking about unnecessary things…"

From her childhood she had been going to Gautam Buddha; then she got married.

Prasenjita had no inclination of that kind but because she was so insistent he said, "It is worth at least one visit to go and see what kind of man this is."

But he was a man of great ego, so he took out the most precious diamond from his treasure to present to Gautam Buddha. He did not want to go there as an ordinary man. Everybody had to know...in fact, he wanted everybody to know, "Who is greater—Gautam Buddha or Prasenjita?" That diamond was so precious that many fights had happened, wars had happened over it.

His wife laughed and she said, "You are absolutely unaware of the man I'm taking you to. It is better that you take a flower rather than a stone to present to him." He could not understand, but he said, "There is no harm, I can take both. Let us see."

When he reached there, he offered his diamond, which he was carrying in one of his hands, and Buddha said simply, "Drop it!" Naturally, what can you do? He dropped it. He thought that perhaps his wife was right. In the other hand he was carrying the lotus, and as he tried to offer the lotus, Buddha said, "Drop it!"

He dropped that too, and became a little afraid: the man seemed to be insane! But ten thousand disciples were there... And Prasenjita stood there thinking that these people must believe that he was stupid. And Buddha said the third time, "Don't you listen to me? Drop it!" Prasenjita thought, "He is really gone. Now I have dropped the diamond, I have dropped the lotus; now I don't have anything."

And at that very moment, Sariputta, an old disciple of Gautam Buddha, started laughing.

His laughter turned Prasenjita towards him, and he asked, "Why are you laughing?"

He said, "You don't understand the language. He is not saying drop the diamond, he is not saying drop the lotus. He is saying drop yourself, drop the ego. You can have the diamond and you can have the lotus, but drop the ego. Don't take it back."

You have heard of Cleopatra, one of the most beautiful women of Egypt. In India, equivalent to Cleopatra, is the beautiful woman contemporary of Gautam Buddha, Amrapali.

Buddha was staying in Vaishali, where Amrapali lived. Amrapali was a prostitute. In Buddha's time in India it was a convention that the most beautiful woman of any city would not be allowed to get married to any one person, because that would create unnecessary jealousy, conflict, fighting. So the most beautiful woman had to become *nagarvadhu*—the wife of the whole town.

It was not disrespectful at all; on the contrary, just as in the contemporary world we declare a beautiful woman as "the Woman of the Year," she was greatly respected. She was not an ordinary prostitute. Her function was that of a prostitute, but she was visited only by the very rich, by kings or princes and generals—the highest strata of society.

Amrapali was very beautiful. One day she was standing on her terrace and she saw a young Buddhist monk. She had never fallen in love with anybody, although every day she had to pretend to be a great lover to this king, to that king, to this rich man, to that general. But she fell suddenly in love with this Buddhist monk who had nothing except a begging bowl—a young man, but of a tremendous presence, awareness, grace. The way he was walking.... She rushed down and asked the monk, "Please—today accept my food."

Other monks were also coming behind him, because whenever Buddha was moving anywhere, ten thousand monks were always moving with him. The other monks could

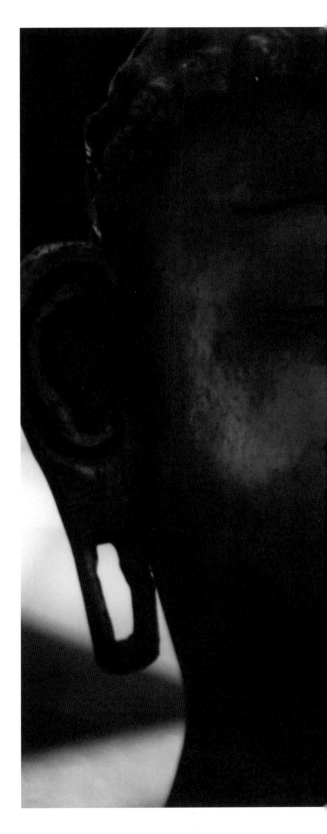

not believe this. They were jealous and angry and feeling all the human qualities and frailties as they saw the young man enter the palace of Amrapali.

Amrapali told him, "After three days the rainy season is going to start..." Buddhist monks don't move for four months when it is the rainy season. Those are the four months they stay in one place; for eight months they continuously move; they can't stay more than three days in one place.

It is a strange psychology: to become attached to some place it takes you at least four days. You can observe it in your own experience. For example, for the first day in a new house you may not be able to sleep, the second day it will be little easier, the third day it will be even easier, and the fourth day you will be able to sleep perfectly at home. So before that time is up, if you are a Buddhist monk, you have to leave.

Amrapali said, "After just three days the rainy season is to begin, and I invite you to stay in my house for the four months."

The young monk said, 'I will ask my master. If he allows me, I will come."

As he went out the crowd of monks asked him what had happened. He said, "I have taken my meal, and the woman has asked me to stay the four months of the rainy season in her palace. I told her that I will ask my master."

The monks were really angry. One day was already too much...but four months! They rushed to find Gautam Buddha. Before the young man could reach the assembly, there were hundreds of monks standing up and telling Gautam Buddha, "This man has to be stopped.

> *If meditation is deep, if awareness is clear, nothing can disturb it*

That woman is a prostitute, and a monk staying four months in a prostitute's house...."

Buddha said, "You keep quiet! Let him come. He has not agreed to stay; he has agreed only if I allow him. Let him come."

The young monk came, touched the feet of Buddha and told the whole story, "The woman is a prostitute, a famous prostitute, Amrapali. She has asked me to stay for four months in her house. Every monk will be staying somewhere, in somebody's house, for the four months. I have told her that I will ask my master, so I am here... whatever you say."

Buddha looked into his eyes and said, "You can stay."

It was a shock. Ten thousand monks. There was great silence...but also great anger, great jealousy. They could not believe that Buddha had allowed a monk to stay in a prostitute's house. After three days the young man left to stay with Amrapali, and the monks every day started bringing gossip: "The whole city is agog. There is only one topic of talk—that a Buddhist monk is staying with Amrapali for four months."

Buddha said, "You should keep silent. Four months will pass, and I trust my monk.

I have looked into his eyes—there was no desire. If I had said no, he would not have felt anything. I said yes... he simply went. And I trust in my monk, in his awareness, in his meditation. "Why are you getting so agitated and worried? If my monk's meditation is deep then he will change Amrapali, and if his meditation is not deep then Amrapali may change him. It is now a question between meditation and a biological attraction. Just wait for four months. I trust this young man. He has been doing perfectly well and I have every certainty he will come out of this fire test absolutely victorious."

Nobody believed Gautam Buddha. His own disciples thought, "He is trusting too much. The man is too young; he is too fresh and Amrapali is much too beautiful. He is taking an unnecessary risk." But there was nothing else to do.

After four months the young man came, touched Buddha's feet—and following him was Amrapali, dressed as a Buddhist nun. She touched Buddha's feet and she said, "I tried my best to seduce your monk, but he seduced me. He convinced me by his presence and awareness that the real life is at your feet. I want to give all my possessions to the commune of your monks."

She had a beautiful garden and a beautiful palace. She said, "You can make it a place where ten thousand monks can stay in any rainy season."

And Buddha said to the assembly, "Now, are you satisfied or not?"

If meditation is deep, if awareness is clear, nothing can disturb it. Then everything is ephemeral. Amrapali became one of the enlightened women among Buddha's disciples.

the last experiment

IT HAPPENED ON the last day of Gautam Buddha's life on earth. A poor man invited him to take his meal at his home. This was the routine: Buddha would open his doors early in the morning and whoever would invite him first, he would accept the invitation for that day. He would go to the house. He used to take only one meal each day.

It was almost impossible for a poor person to invite him; it was accidental. The king was coming to invite him, but on the way an accident happened and the chariot in which he was coming broke down, so he was delayed. He reached there just a few minutes late. By that time Buddha had already accepted the invitation of the poor man.

The king said, "I know this man. He has been trying his whole life to invite you whenever you come to this town."

Buddha loved a few places very well. Vaishali, one of the cities, was one of his favorites. In his forty-two years as a master he visited Vaishali at least forty times, almost every year. He remained in Vaishali for at least twelve rainy seasons, because in the rainy season it was too difficult to walk.

So for three or four months he would remain in one place and for eight months he would move around.

The places where Buddha moved are in Bihar. The name *Bihar* comes from Buddha's movements and means "the place where a buddha travels." The boundary of this area, where for forty-two years he continuously traveled, defines the whole state of Bihar.

The king said, "I know this man, I have seen him many times. He is always trying...yet he has nothing to offer! Please reject this idea of going to his house."

But Buddha said, "That is impossible. I cannot reject the invitation. I have to go." So he went. And his going became fatal to his body, because in Bihar the poor men collect mushrooms, dry them, and keep them for the rainy season. They use them as vegetables. Sometimes mushrooms are poisonous. And he had prepared mushrooms for Buddha—he had nothing else, just rice and mushrooms.

Buddha looked at what he offered him, but saying no to the poor man would hurt him, so he ate the mushrooms. They were very bitter, but to say that would hurt the poor man, so he ate them all without saying anything, thanked the man, and left. He died of food poisoning.

When he was asked at the last moment, "Why did you accept? You knew, the king had warned you, other disciples were warning you that he is so poor, he would not be able to offer you the right food. And you are old, eighty-two years old—you need the right nourishment. But you didn't listen."

Buddha said, "It was impossible. Whenever truth is invited it has to accept. And he invited me with such passion and love as nobody has ever invited me—it was worth risking my life."

This story is beautiful. It is true about the ultimate truth, also: all that is needed on our part is a total invitation, not holding back even a small part of our being. If we are available, open, ready to receive the host, the host comes. It has never been otherwise.

This is the law of existence: truth cannot be conquered but it can be invited. One has to be a host for the ultimate guest. That's what I call meditation; it makes you empty of all rubbish, it empties you completely so you become spacious, receptive, sensitive, vulnerable, available. And all those qualities make you passionately inviting—an invitation for the unknown, an invitation for the unnamable, an invitation for that which will make your life a fulfillment, without which life is just an exercise in utter futility. But one cannot do anything more than that: just offer an invitation and wait.

This is what I call prayer: an invitation and waiting in deep trust that it is going to happen. And it happens, it has always happened! *Aes dhammo sanantano*, says Buddha—this is the ultimate law of existence.

The day Buddha died, in the morning he gathered all his disciples, all his sannyasins, and told them,

> *This is the law of existence: truth cannot be conquered but it can be invited*

"The last day has come now, my boat has arrived and I have to leave. This has been a beautiful journey, a beautiful togetherness. If you have any questions to ask, you can ask them, because I will not be available to you physically anymore."

A great silence fell on the disciples, a great sadness. And Buddha laughed and said, "Don't be sad, because that's what I have been teaching you again and again—everything that begins, ends. Now let me teach you by my death too. As I have been teaching you through my life, let me teach you through my death, too."

Nobody could gather the courage to ask a question. Their whole life they had asked thousands and thousands of questions, and this was not a moment to ask anything; they were not in the mood, they were crying and weeping.

So Buddha said, "Goodbye. If you don't have any questions then I will depart." He sat under the tree with closed eyes and he disappeared from the body. In the Buddhist tradition, this is called "the first meditation"—to disappear from the body. It means to disidentify

> *He is no longer a person, no longer a form, no longer a wave; he disappears into the ocean*

yourself from the body, to know totally and absolutely, "I am not the body."

A question is bound to arise in your mind: had Buddha not known it before? He had known it before, but a person like Buddha then has to create some device so that just a little bit of him remains connected with the body. Otherwise he would have died long before—forty-two years before he would have died. The day his enlightenment happened, he would have died. Out of compassion he created a desire, the desire to help people. It is a desire, and it keeps you attached to the body. He created a desire to help people. "Whatsoever I have known, I have to share."

If you want to share, you will have to use the mind and the body. That small part remained attached. Now he cuts even that small root in the body; he becomes disidentified from the body. The first meditation complete, the body is left.

Then the second meditation: the mind is dropped. He had dropped the mind long before; it was dropped as a master, but as

a servant it was still used. Now it is not even needed as a servant, it is utterly dropped, totally dropped.

And then the third meditation: he dropped his heart. It had been needed up to now, he had been functioning through his heart; otherwise, compassion would not have been possible. He had been the heart; now he disconnects from the heart.

When these three meditations are completed, the fourth happens. He is no longer a person, no longer a form, no longer a wave; he disappears into the ocean. He becomes that which he had always been, he becomes that which he had known forty-two years before but had been somehow managing to delay in order to help people.

His death is a tremendous experiment in meditation. It is said that many who were present first saw that the body was no longer the same; something had happened, the aliveness had disappeared from the body. The body was there, but like a statue. Those who were more perceptive, more meditative, immediately saw that now the mind had been dropped and there was no mind inside. Those who were even more perceptive could see that the heart was finished. And those who were on the verge of buddhahood, seeing Buddha disappear, they also disappeared.

Many disciples became enlightened the day Buddha died, many—just seeing him dying. They had watched him living, they had seen his life, but now came the crescendo, the climax. They saw him dying such a beautiful death with such grace, such meditativeness… seeing it, many were awakened.

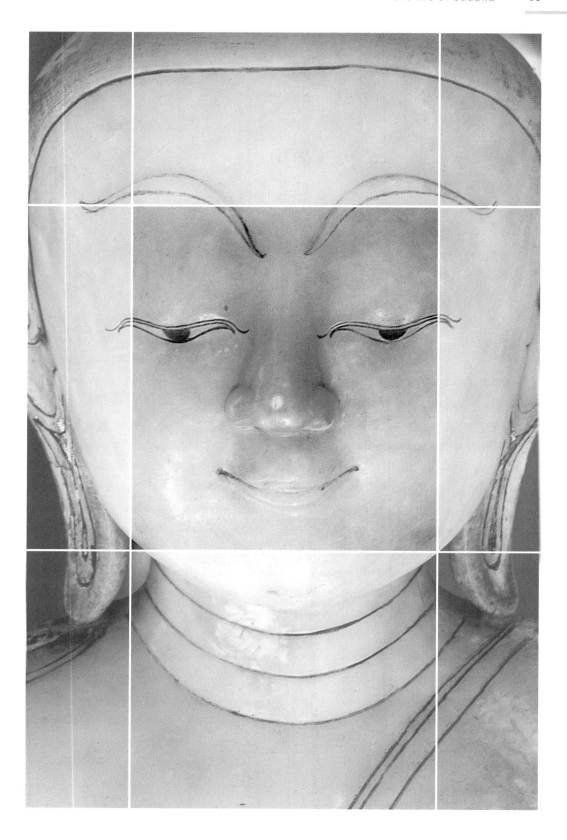

the
teachings

Before enlightenment the master prepares the people who are going to succeed him, makes them more articulate, makes them better able to transform the wordless into words, the absolutely silent into song, the absolutely unmoving into dance.

I have heard

Once Gautam Buddha was passing through a forest and it was the season of autumn. The forest was full of dry leaves, and Ananda, finding him alone, said to him, "I have always wanted to ask, but before the others I could not dare. Just tell me the truth: have you told us everything that you know or are you still holding back a few secrets?"

GAUTAM BUDDHA took a handful of leaves from the ground and said to Ananda, "I have told you only this much—the leaves that you see in my hand—but that which I know is as vast as all the leaves in this great forest. It is not that I want to hold it back, but it is simply impossible! Even to talk about a few leaves is an arduous effort, because it simply goes above your head. You know thoughts, but you have never experienced thoughtlessness. You know emotions, but you have never known a state where all emotions are absent, just as if all the clouds in the sky have disappeared.

"So I am trying my best," he said, "but more than this is not possible to transfer through words. If I can make you understand only this much: that there is much more to life than words can contain; if I can convince you that there is something more than your mind knows, that's enough. Then the seed is sown."

Gautam Buddha, in his whole life, never allowed people to write down what he was saying. His reason was that if you are writing it down, your attention becomes divided. You are no longer total. You have to hear and you have to write, and what he is saying is so subtle that unless you are total, you are going to miss it. So rather than writing it down, try with your totality and intensity to approach your heart, to let it sink within you.

He spoke for forty-two years. After his death, the first task was to write down whatever the disciples remembered; otherwise, it would have been lost to humanity.

They did a great service and also a great disservice. They wrote things down, but they came to see a strange phenomenon—everybody had heard something different. Their memory, their remembrance, was not the same.

Thirty-two schools sprang up, proclaiming, "This is what Buddha has said." Only one man—a man to be remembered forever, his closest disciple, Ananda—who was not even enlightened before Buddha died, out of his humbleness, knew, "I was unenlightened, how can I hear exactly what comes from an enlightened consciousness? I am going to interpret it, I am going to mix it with my own thoughts, I am going to give it my own color, my own nuance. It cannot carry within me the same meaning it has brought, because I don't have yet those eyes that can see and those ears that can hear." Out of this humbleness, the things that he remembered and wrote down became the basic scriptures of Buddhism. They all start with "I have heard Gautam Buddha say..."

All thirty-two philosophical schools—they were led by great scholars, far greater than Ananda, far more capable of interpreting, of bringing meanings to things, of making systems out of words—those thirty-two schools slowly, slowly were rejected. The reason for their rejection was that they had missed a single qualification: "I have heard...." They were saying,

"Gautam Buddha said..." and the emphasis was on Gautam Buddha.

Ananda's version is the universally accepted version. Strange...there were enlightened people, but they remained silent because what they had heard was not possible to express. And there were unenlightened, philosophical geniuses, who were articulate and wrote great treatises—but they were not accepted. And the man who was not enlightened, not a great philosopher, just a humble caretaker of Gautam Buddha—his words have been accepted. The reason is his beginning: "I have heard... I don't know whether he was saying it or not. I cannot impose myself on him. All that I can say is what echoed in me. I can talk about my mind—not the silence of Gautam Buddha."

big boat, little boat

BEFORE ENLIGHTENMENT the master prepares the people who are going to succeed him, makes them more articulate, makes them better able to transform the wordless into words, the absolutely silent into song, the absolutely unmoving into dance. Only then will he be able to convey something of help to blind humanity.

Buddha divided his enlightened people into two categories. They both have the same height—there is no quality of lower or higher—they both belong to the same cosmic reality, the fundamental nature. One category is called the *arhatas*—the arhatas are the ones who become enlightened and remain silent—and the second category is called *bodhisattvas*. They also become enlightened, but their work is to convey something, some device, some hint about their experience to people.

Arhatas are also called *hinayana*, a little boat in which one man can row and go to the other side. Of course he reaches the other shore. And bodhisattvas are the *mahayana*, a great ship in which thousands of people can move to the other shore. The other shore is the same, but the bodhisattva helps many.

The arhata is not articulate; he is a simple, nice, utterly humble person, but will not utter a single word of what he has attained. It is too much for him to say anything. He is completely contented; why should he speak? And anyway, everybody has to find his own way, so why unnecessarily harass people? The arhata has his own standpoint.

The arhata is someone who makes every effort to become enlightened and once he is enlightened he completely forgets about those who are still groping in the dark. He has no concern with others. It is enough for him to become enlightened. In fact, according to the arhatas, even the great idea of compassion is nothing but another kind of attachment.

Compassion is also a relationship; howsoever beautiful and great, it is also a concern with others. It is also a desire. Although it is a good desire, it makes no difference—according to the arhatas, desire is a bondage whether it is good or bad. The chains can be made of gold or of steel, it doesn't matter; chains are chains. Compassion is a golden chain.

The arhata insists that nobody can help anybody else at all. The very idea of helping others is based on wrong foundations. You can help only yourself.

It may occur to the ordinary mind that the arhata is very selfish. But if you look without any prejudice, perhaps he also has something immensely important to declare to the world. Even helping the other is an interference in his life, in his lifestyle, in his destiny, in his future. Hence, arhatas don't believe in compassion. Compassion to them is another beautiful desire to keep you tethered to the world of attachments. It is another name—beautiful, but it is still just a name—for a desiring mind.

Why should you be interested in somebody becoming enlightened? It is none of your business. Everybody has absolute freedom to be himself. The arhata insists on individuality and its absolute freedom. Even for the sake of good, nobody can be allowed to interfere in anybody else's life.

Hence the moment he becomes enlightened, the arhata does not accept disciples, he never preaches, he never helps in any way. He simply lives in his ecstasy. If somebody on his own can drink out of his well, he will not prevent him, but he will not send an invitation. If you come to him on your own accord and sit by his side and drink his presence and get on the path, that is your business. If you go astray, he will not stop you.

In a certain way this is the greatest respect ever paid to individual freedom—to the logical extreme. Even if you are falling into deep darkness, the arhata will silently wait. If his presence can help, that is okay, but he is not going to move his hands to help you, give you a hand, pull you out of a ditch. You are free to fall in a ditch and if you can fall in a ditch, you are absolutely capable of getting out of it. The very idea of compassion is foreign to the philosophy of the *arhatas*.

Gautam Buddha accepted that there are a few people who will become arhatas, and their path will be called *hinayana* —"the small vehicle"—the small boat in which only one person can go to the other shore. The *arhata* does not create a big ship or collect a crowd in

a Noah's Ark to take them to the further shore. He goes by himself in his small boat, which cannot even contain two. He is born alone in the world, he has lived and died millions of times alone in the world, and alone he is going to the universal source.

Buddha accepts and respects the way of the *arhata*, but he also knows there are people who have immense compassion and when they become enlightened, their first longing is to share their joy, to share their truth. Compassion is their way. They also have a profound truth. These people are the *bodhisattvas*. They provoke and invite others to the same experience. And they wait on this shore as long as possible to help all seekers who are ready to move on the path, and who just need a guide, a helping hand. The *bodhisattvas* can postpone going to the far shore out of compassion for blind people groping in darkness.

Buddha had such a comprehensive and vast perception that he accepted both—that it is the nature of a few people to be arhatas, and it is also the nature of other people to be bodhisattvas. It is the standpoint of Gautam Buddha that such is the case and nothing can be

done about it—an arhata will be an arhata and a bodhisattva will be a bodhisattva. Their natures have different destinies, although they reach the same goal finally. But after reaching the goal there is a parting of the ways.

The arhatas don't stay on this shore even for a single moment. They are tired, they have been long enough in this wheel of *samsara*, moving through birth and death millions of times. It has already been too much. They are bored and don't want to stay even a single minute more. Their boat has arrived, and immediately they start moving toward the further shore. This is their suchness.

Then there are bodhisattvas who tell the boatman, "Wait, there is no hurry. I have lingered on this shore long enough—in misery, in suffering, in anguish, in agony. Now all that has disappeared. I am in absolute bliss, silence, and peace, and I don't see that there is anything more on the other shore. So as long as I can manage, I will be here to help people."

Gautam Buddha was certainly one of those people who can see the truth even in contradictions. He accepted both without making anybody feel lower or higher.

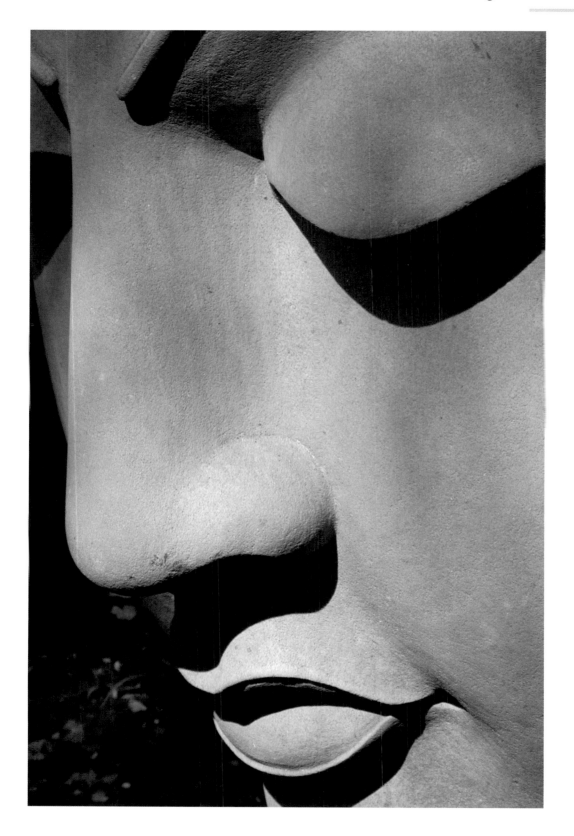

s u c h n e s s

TRY TO UNDERSTAND the word *suchness*. Buddha depends on that word. In Buddha's own language it is *tathata*—suchness. The whole Buddhist meditation consists of living in this word, living with this word, so deeply that the word disappears and you become the suchness.

For example, you are ill. The attitude of suchness is: accept it—and say to yourself, "Such is the way of the body," or, "Things are such." Don't create a fight, don't start struggling. You have a headache—accept it. Such is the nature of things. Suddenly there is a change, because when this attitude comes in, a change follows just like a shadow. If you can accept your headache, the headache disappears.

Try it. If you accept a discomfort, it starts dispersing. Why does this happen? It happens because whenever you are fighting, your energy is divided: half the energy moving into discomfort, the headache, and half the energy fighting the headache—a rift, a gap, and thus the fight. Really, this fight is a deeper headache. Once you accept, once you don't complain, once you don't fight, the energy becomes one within. The rift is bridged, and so much energy is released because now there is no conflict that the release of energy itself becomes a healing force.

Healing doesn't come from outside. All that medicine can do is to help the body bring its own healing force into action. All that a doctor can do is to help you find your own healing power. Health cannot be forced from outside; it is your energy flowering.

This word *suchness* can work so deeply with physical illness, with mental illness, and finally with spiritual illness—this is a secret method—that they all dissolve. Start with the body, because that is the lowest layer. If you succeed there, then higher levels can be tried. If you fail there, then it will be difficult for you to move higher.

Something is wrong in the body: relax and accept it, and simply say inside—not only in words, but also feel it deeply—"such is the nature of things."

A body is a compound with many things combined in it. The body is born, it is prone to death. It is a mechanism, and complex; there is every possibility of something or other going wrong. Accept it, and don't be identified. When you accept you remain above, you remain beyond. When you fight you come down to the same level. Acceptance is transcendence.

When you accept, you are on a hill; the body is left behind. You say, "Yes, such is the nature of it. Things born will have to die. And if things born have to die, they will be ill sometimes. Nothing to be worried about too much"—as if it is not happening to you, just happening in the world of things. This is the beauty: when you are not fighting, you transcend. You are no longer on the same level. This transcendence becomes a healing force. Suddenly the body starts changing.

The same happens to mental worries, tensions, anxieties, anguish. You are worried about a certain thing. What is the worry? You cannot accept the fact; that's the worry. You would like it in some way to be different from how it is happening. You are worried because you have some ideas to enforce on nature.

you can come to her and hide from the world. You can rely on her; she will be there. Even if the whole world is against you, she will not be against you; she is a consolation. Now she is leaving, what will happen to you? Suddenly you are in a panic, worried.

What are you saying? What are you saying with your worry? You are saying that you cannot accept this happening, this should not be so. You expected it otherwise, just the contrary; you wanted this wife to be yours forever and ever, and now she is leaving.

But what can you do? When love disappears what can you do? There is no way; you cannot force love, you cannot force this wife to remain with you. Rather, you can force—that's what many people are doing—you can force her to stay. The dead body will be there, but the living spirit will have left. Then *that* will be a tension for you.

Against nature, nothing can be done. Love was a flowering, but now the flower has faded. The breeze came into your house, now it has moved into another. Such is the way of things, they go on moving and changing. The world of things is in flux, nothing is permanent there. Don't expect! If you expect permanency in a world where everything is impermanent, you will create worry.

You would like this love to be forever. Nothing can be forever in this world—all that belongs to this world is momentary. This is the nature of things, suchness, *tathata*. So you know now the love has disappeared. It gives you sadness—accept sadness. You feel trembling—accept trembling, don't suppress it. You feel like crying, cry. Accept it! Don't force it, don't put on

For example, you are getting old. You are worried. You would like to remain young forever—this is the worry. You love your wife, you depend on her, and she is thinking of leaving, or moving in with another man, and you are worried—worried because what will happen to you? You depend on her so much, you feel so much security with her. When she is gone there will be no security. She has not only been a wife to you, she has been a mother also, a shelter;

a face; don't pretend that you are not worried, because that won't help. If you are worried, you are worried. If the wife is leaving, she is leaving. If the love is no more, it is no more. You cannot fight the fact; you have to accept it.

If you accept it grudgingly, then you will be continually in pain and suffering. If you accept it without any complaint—not in helplessness, but in understanding—it becomes suchness. Then you are no longer worried, then there is no problem. The problem arose not because of the fact, but because you couldn't accept it the way it was happening. You wanted it to follow your idea.

Remember, life is not going to follow you—you have to follow life. Grudgingly or happily, that's your choice. If you follow grudgingly you will be in suffering. If you follow happily you become a buddha, your life becomes an ecstasy.

Buddha also has to die—things won't change specially for him—but he dies in a different way. He dies so happily, as if there is no death. He simply disappears, because he says, "Anything that is born is going to die. Birth implies death, so it is okay, nothing can be done about it."

You can be miserable and die. Then you miss the point, the beauty that death can give to you, the grace that happens in the last moment, the illumination that happens when body and soul part. You will miss that because you are so worried, and you are clinging to the past so much, and to the body, and your eyes are closed. You cannot see what is happening because you cannot accept it. So you close your eyes, you close your whole being and you die—you will die many times, and you will go on missing the point of it.

> **Remember, life is not going to follow you—you have to follow life**

Death is beautiful if you can accept, if you can open the door with a welcoming heart, a warm reception: "Yes, because if I am born I am going to die. So the day has come, the circle becomes complete." You receive death as a guest, a welcome guest, and the quality of the phenomenon changes immediately. Suddenly you are deathless: the body is dying, you are not dying. You can see it now—only the clothes are dropping, not you. Only the cover, the container, not the content; the consciousness remains in its illumination. More so, because in life, many were the covers on your consciousness. In death it is naked. And when consciousness is totally naked it has a splendor of its own; it is the most beautiful thing in the world.

But for that, an attitude of suchness has to be imbibed. When I say imbibed, I mean imbibed—not just as a mental thought, not the "philosophy of suchness," but your whole way of life becomes suchness. You don't even think about it; it simply becomes natural.

You eat in suchness, you sleep in suchness, you breathe in suchness. You love in suchness, you weep in suchness. It becomes your lifestyle. You need not bother about it, you need not think about it; it is the way you are. That is what

I mean by the word *imbibe*. You imbibe it, you digest it. It flows in your blood, it goes deep into your bones; it reaches to the very beat of your heart. You accept.

The word *accept* is not very good. It is loaded—because of you, not because of the word—because you accept only when you feel helpless. You accept grudgingly, you accept halfheartedly. You accept only when you cannot do anything else. But deep down you still wish it were otherwise; you would have been happy if it had been otherwise. You accept like a beggar, not like a king—and the difference is great.

If your wife or husband leaves, finally you come to accept it. What can be done? You weep and cry, and many nights you brood and worry, and many nightmares are around you, and suffering...and then what to do? Time heals, not understanding. Time—and remember, time is needed only because you are not understanding. Otherwise *instant* healing happens. Time is needed because you are not understanding. So, by and by—six months, eight months, a year— things become dim, they are lost in the memory, covered with much dust. And the gap grows over one year; by and by you forget.

Still, sometimes the wound hurts. Sometimes a woman passes on the road and suddenly you remember. Some similarity, the way she walks, and the wife is remembered— and the wound. Then you fall in love with someone. Then more dust gathers, the less you remember. But even with a new woman, sometimes the way she looks...and your wife comes to mind. The way she sings in the bathroom...and the memory surfaces and the wound is there, green.

It hurts because you carry the past. You carry everything; that's why you are so burdened. You carry everything! You were a child; the child is still there, you are carrying it. You were a young man; the young man is still there with all his wounds, experiences, stupidities—he is there. You carry your whole past, layers upon layers—everything is there.

That's why you sometimes regress. If something happens and you feel helpless, you start crying like a child. You have regressed in time, the child has taken over. The child is more efficient in weeping than you, so the child comes in and takes over and you start crying and weeping. You can even start kicking, just like a child in a tantrum. But everything is there.

Why is so much load carried? Because you never really accepted anything. Listen—if you accept something it never becomes a load; the wound is not carried. You accepted the phenomenon; there is nothing to carry from it, you are out of it. Through acceptance you are out of it. Through half-hearted, helpless acceptance, it is carried.

Remember one thing: Anything incomplete is carried by the mind forever and forever. Anything complete is dropped. Mind has a tendency to carry the incomplete things in the hope that some day there may be an opportunity to complete them. You are still waiting for the wife to come back, or for the husband, or for the days that have gone—you are still waiting. You have not transcended the past. And because of such a loaded past, you cannot live in the present. Your present is a mess because of the past, and your future is going to be the same—because the past will become

COMPLETE CONTENTMENT

When you accept everything, your life becomes cheerful. Nobody can make you miserable, no thing can make you miserable.

A man with three hairs on his otherwise bald head came into a hair salon and asked to get his hair shampooed and braided. The hairdresser got on with his job but just as he was about to finish combing it, one of the hairs fell out.

The hairdresser was very embarrassed, but the man only said, "Well, what to do? I guess I will have to part my hair in the middle!"

The hairdresser very carefully put one hair to the right side and was about to put the other to the left side when that one fell out too. The hairdresser could not apologize enough but the man took it calmly.

"Well," he said, "I guess now I will have to run around with my hair all ruffled up."

This is *tathata*, this is total acceptance! You cannot disturb such a man. He is always contented, always finds a way to be contented. It is a great art. And a man who always finds a way to remain contented has the capacity to see things transparently.

Discontent clouds your eyes and your vision; contentment makes your eyes unclouded and your vision clear. You can see through and through; you can understand things as they are.

more and more heavy. Every day it is becoming heavier and heavier.

When you really accept, in that attitude of suchness there is no grudge, you are not helpless. Simply you understand that this is the nature of things.

For example, if I want to go out of the room, I will go out through the door, not through the wall, because to enter the wall will mean hitting my head against it. It is foolish. It is the nature of the wall to hinder, so you don't try to pass through it! It is the nature of the door that you pass through it; because the door is empty, you can pass through it.

When a buddha accepts, he accepts things like the wall and the door. He passes through the door, as that is the only way. First you try to pass through the wall, and you wound yourself in millions of ways. And when you cannot get out—crushed, defeated, depressed, fallen—then you crawl toward the door. You could have gone through the door in the first place! Why did you try to start fighting with the wall?

If you can look at things with clarity, you won't do things like this—trying to make a door out of a wall? If love disappears, it has disappeared! Now there is a wall; don't try to go through it. Now the door is no longer there, the heart is no longer there; the heart has opened to somebody else. You are not alone here; there are others also. The door is no more—for you, it has become a wall. Don't try, and don't knock your head against it. You will be wounded unnecessarily. And wounded, defeated, even the door will not be such a beautiful thing to pass through.

Simply look at things. If something is natural, don't try to force any unnatural thing on it.

Choose the door and be out of it. If you are every day trying the foolishness of passing through the wall, then you become tense and you feel constant confusion. Anguish becomes your very life, the core of it.

Why not look at the facts as they are? Why can't you look at the facts? Because your wishes are too great. You go on hoping against all hope.

Just look: Whenever there is a situation, don't desire anything, because desire will lead you astray. Don't wish and don't imagine. Simply look at the fact with your total consciousness available...and suddenly a door opens. You never move through the wall, you move through the door, unscratched. Then you remain unburdened.

Remember, suchness is an understanding, not a helpless fate. That's the difference. There are people who believe in fate, destiny. They say, "What can you do? God has willed it in such a way. My young child has died, so it is God's will and this is my fate. It was written, it was going to happen."

However, deep down there is rejection. These are just tricks to polish the rejection. Do you know God? Do you know fate? Do you know that it was written? No, these are all rationalizations—ideas that you use just to console yourself.

The attitude of suchness is not a fatalist attitude. It does not bring in God, or fate, or destiny—nothing. It says, "Simply look at things. Simply look at the facticity of things, understand. And there is a door, there is always a door." You transcend.

Suchness means acceptance with a total, welcoming heart, not in helplessness.

the middle way

GAUTAM BUDDHA was the first man to use the words "to be in the middle," and of course nobody has been able to improve upon the meanings that he gave to the word *middle*.

He called his path the middle path. The first meaning is that if you can avoid both the extremes, the rightist and the leftist—if you can be exactly in the middle of both the extremes, you will not be in the middle, you will have transcended the whole trinity of extremes, *and* the middle. If you drop both the extremes, the middle disappears on its own accord. Middle of what...?

Gautam Buddha's insistence on the middle is not on the middle itself; it is, in fact, a subtle way to persuade you for transformation. But to tell you directly to be transformed may make you apprehensive, afraid. To be in the middle seems to be very simple.

> *Existence is an organic unity. It does not exclude anything; it is all-inclusive*

Gautam Buddha played with the word out of sheer compassion. His own term for the middle is *majjhim nikaya*, the middle path. Every extreme has to exclude the other extreme; every extreme has to be in opposition to the other polarity. The negative is against the positive, the minus is against the plus, death is against life. If you take them as extremes, they naturally appear as opposites.

But the man who can stop exactly in the middle immediately transcends all the extremes and the middle together. From the higher standpoint of the transformed being, you can see there is no opposition at all. The extremes are not opposites, not contradictories, but only complementaries.

Life and death are not enemies, they are part of one single process. Death does not end life, it simply renews it. It gives it a new form, a new body, a new plane of consciousness. It is not against life; looked at rightly, it is a process of refreshing life, of rejuvenating life. The day is not against the night....

In existence there is no opposition in anything; all opposites contribute to the whole. Existence is an organic unity. It does not exclude anything; it is all-inclusive.

The man who can stop in the middle comes to know this tremendous experience, that there are no opposites, no contradictories. The whole existence is one, and in that oneness all contradictions, all oppositions, all contraries

disappear into a single unity. Then life includes death, then day includes night. A man who can experience this organic unity becomes fearless, becomes without any anguish or angst. For the first time he realizes his vastness—he is as vast as the whole of existence. The moment somebody transcends the opposites and comes to know them as complementaries, he is not only part of the whole, he becomes the whole.

Let me tell you the final absurdity. Once in a while—in someone like Gautam Buddha, or Manavira, or Chuang Tzu, or Lao Tzu—it happens that the part becomes *bigger* than the whole. Absolutely illogical, absolutely unmathematical—but still absolutely right. A Gautam Buddha not only contains the whole, but because of his transformation he is a little bit more than the whole. The whole is not aware of its complementariness. Gautam Buddha is aware of its complementariness, and that's where he transcends and becomes bigger than the whole, although he is still a part of it. To be

in the middle is one of the great methods of transforming yourself into the ultimate. To prepare yourself for being in the middle you will have to drop all extremist ideas. And all your ideas are extremist—either leftist or rightist, either Christian or Mohammedan, either Hindu or Buddhist. You have chosen; you have not allowed a choiceless consciousness, accepting everything that is.

All your prejudices are your choices. I am against all your prejudices, in order to bring you into the middle.

The pope heard that a certain lady in Ireland had produced ten children, so he sent one of his cardinals to grant her his blessings.

When he met the lady, the cardinal was disgusted to learn that she was not a Catholic. "Do you mean to say," he thundered, "that I have come all this way to meet a sex-mad Protestant?"

This is the way of all prejudices. A *sannyasin* is one who has no prejudices, who has not chosen any ideology to be his own, who is choicelessly aware of all that is. In this choicelessness you will be in the middle. The moment you choose, you choose some extreme. The moment you choose, you choose against something; otherwise there is no question of choice. Being in a choiceless awareness is another meaning of being in the middle.

It happened that a very beautiful young prince—his name was Shrona—listened for the first time to Gautam Buddha. Buddha was visiting the capital of the young man's kingdom, and listening to Gautam Buddha, the prince immediately asked to be initiated. He was well known as a sitar player and he was also well known for luxurious living, utterly luxurious.

It was said that even when he was going upstairs, rather than having a railing on the staircase, naked, beautiful women used to stand all along the staircase so that he could move from one woman's shoulder to another woman's shoulder. That was his way to go upstairs. He used to sleep the whole day because the hangover of the night before was too much; the whole night was a night of celebrations, drinking, eating, music, dance. There was no time for him to sleep in the night.

All these things were well known to the people. Gautam Buddha had never hesitated to give initiation to any man before. Now he hesitated. He said, "Shrona, I know everything about you; I would like you to reconsider; think it over. I am still going to stay in this capital for the four months of the rainy season."

For four months, in the rainy season, Gautam Buddha never used to move around, nor did his sannyasins. Eight months of the year they were continuously wandering and sharing their experiences of meditation and higher states of consciousness. But because twenty-five centuries ago there were only mud roads and Buddha had not allowed his disciples to have any possessions—not even an umbrella, no shoes, and just three pieces of cloth. One was

for any emergency, and two so that you could change every day after the bath; more than three were not allowed. In the rainy season when it was pouring it would have been difficult to keep those three cloths dry, and to walk in the mud in the pouring rain might make many people sick.

For that reason he had made it a point that for four months you remain in one place, and those who want to see you can come. Eight months you should go to every thirsty person; for four months let others come to you.

So he said, "There is no hurry, Shrona."

But Shrona said, "Once I have made a decision I never reconsider. You have to give me initiation right now."

Buddha still tried to persuade him: "There is no harm in reconsidering it, because you have lived a life of utter luxury. You have never walked on the road, you have been always in a golden chariot. You have never come out of your luxurious palace and gardens. You have lived continuously with beautiful women, with great musicians, with dancers. All that will not be possible when you become a *sannyasin*." He told Shrona, "You will not be able. And I don't like anybody to return to the world, because that makes him lose his self-respect. That's why I tell you to consider...."

Shrona said, "I have considered again and again and I still want to be *initiated* right now. The more you tell me to consider the more I become adamant and stubborn."

Gautam Buddha had to relent and give him initiation, and from the second day there was trouble, but trouble that no *sannyasin* of Gautam Buddha had expected. A trouble

that perhaps Gautam Buddha had expected started happening.

When all the monks had three pieces of cloth, Shrona started living naked—from one extreme to the other extreme. When all the Buddhist bhikkus were walking on the road, Shrona would always walk by the side of the road in the thorns. When the other monks were resting under the shade of the trees, Shrona would always stand in the hot sun in the middle of the day.

Within six months the beautiful young prince became almost old, a skeleton, black; one could not recognize that this was the man who used to be a great prince and was famous for his luxurious life. His feet were bleeding, his whole body had shrunk, and one night after six months Gautam Buddha went to the tree under which he was sleeping. It is one of the rare occasions when Buddha went in the night to any *sannyasin* for any reason. There is no other incident, at least in the Buddhist scriptures. This is the only incident.

He woke Shrona up and asked him a strange question: "I have heard that when you were a prince you were also the greatest sitarist in the country. Is that right?"

Shrona said, "You could have asked at any time. I don't see the point in the middle of the night."

Gautam Buddha said, "Just wait a little, you will see the point."

Shrona said, "Yes, it is true."

Buddha said, "Now the second question is, if the strings of the sitar are too tight, will there be any music born out of those strings?"

Shrona said, "Of course not. If they are too tight they will be broken."

> *Always find the middle and you have found the path of meditation and the path of liberation*

Buddha said, "If they are too loose, will there be any music?"

Shrona said, "You are asking strange questions in the middle of the night. When the strings are too loose they cannot create any music. A certain tension is needed. In fact to play on a sitar is simple. The real mastery is to keep the strings exactly in the middle, neither too tight nor too loose."

Buddha said, "This is the point I came to make to you. Life is also a musical instrument: too tight and there is no music, too loose and there is no music. The strings of life have to be exactly in the middle, neither too tight nor too loose only then is there music. And only a master knows how to keep them in the middle. Because you have been a master sitarist I would like you also to become a master of life. Don't move from one extreme to another, from luxury to austerity, from pleasures to self-torture. Try to be exactly in the middle."

Gautam Buddha in a sense is one of the most profound psychologists that the world has produced. To be in the middle in every action of your life—always find the middle and you have found the path of meditation and the path of liberation.

right mindfulness

A HUMAN IS A CROWD, a crowd of many voices—relevant, irrelevant, consistent, inconsistent—each voice pulling in its own way; all the voices pulling the individual apart. Ordinarily, a human is a mess, virtually a kind of madness. You somehow manage to look sane. Deep down, layers and layers of insanity are boiling within you. They can erupt any moment, your control can be lost any moment, because your control is enforced from without. It is not a discipline that has come from your center of being.

For social reasons, economic reasons, political reasons, you have enforced a certain character upon yourself. But many vital forces exist against that character within you. They are continuously sabotaging your character. Hence, every day you commit many mistakes, many errors. Even sometimes you feel that you never wanted to do it. In spite of yourself, you go on committing many mistakes—because you are not one, you are many.

Buddha does not call these mistakes sins, because to call them sin would be condemning. He simply calls them misdemeanors, mistakes, errors. To err is human, not to err is divine, and the way from the human to the divine goes through mindfulness. These many voices within you can stop torturing you, pulling you, pushing you. These many voices can disappear if you become mindful.

In a mindful state mistakes are not committed—not that you control them, but in a mindful state, in an alert, aware state, voices, many voices cease—you become one, and whatsoever you do comes from the core of your being. It is never wrong. This has to be understood.

In the modern Human Potential Movement is a parallel to help you understand it. That's what Transactional Analysis calls the triangle of PAC. P means parent, A means adult, C means child. These are your three layers, as if you are a three-storied building.

The first floor is that of the child, the second floor is that of the parent, the third floor is that of the adult. All three exist together. This is your inner triangle and conflict. Your child says one thing, your parent says something else, and your adult, rational mind says something else.

The child says, "Enjoy." For the child this moment is the only moment; he has no other considerations. The child is spontaneous, but unaware of the consequences—unaware of past, unaware of future. He lives in the moment. He has no values and he has no mindfulness, no awareness. The child consists of felt concepts; he lives through feeling. His whole being is irrational.

Of course he comes into many conflicts with others. He comes into many contradictions within himself, because one feeling helps him to do one thing, then suddenly he starts feeling another emotion. A child never can complete anything. By the time he can complete it, his feeling has changed. He starts many things but never comes to any conclusion. A child remains inconclusive. He enjoys, but his enjoyment is not creative, cannot be creative. He delights, but life cannot be lived only through delight. You cannot remain a child forever. You will have to learn many things, because you are not alone here.

If you were alone then there would be no question—you could have remained a child forever. But the society is there, millions of people are there; you have to follow many rules, you have to hold many values. Otherwise, there would be so much conflict that life would become impossible. The child has to be disciplined, and that's where the parent comes in.

The parental voice in you is the voice of the society, culture, civilization; the voice that makes you capable of living in a world where you are not alone, where there are many individuals with conflicting ambitions, where there is much struggle for survival, where there is much conflict. You have to pave your path, and you have to move cautiously.

The parental voice is that of caution. It makes you civilized. The child is wild; the parental voice helps you to become civilized. The word *civil* is good. It means one who has become capable of living in a city; who has become capable of being a member of a group, of a society.

The child is very dictatorial. The child thinks he is the center of the world. The parents have to teach you that you are not the center of the

world—everybody thinks that way. They have to make you more and more alert that there are many people in the world and you are not alone. You have to consider them if you want to be considered by them. Otherwise, you will be crushed. It is a sheer question of survival, of policy, of politics.

The parental voice gives you some commandments—what to do, what not to do. The parent makes you cautious. It is needed.

And then there is the third voice within you, the third layer when you have become adult

and you are no longer controlled by your parents; your own reason has come of age and you can think on your own.

The child consists of felt concepts; the parent consists of taught concepts; and the adult consists of thought concepts. These three layers are continuously in conflict. The child says one thing, the parent says the opposite, and reason may say something totally different.

You see beautiful food. The child says to eat as much as you want. The parental voice says that many things have to be considered—whether you are feeling hungry, whether the smell or the taste of the food is its only appeal. Is this food really nutritious? Is it going to nourish your body or can it become harmful to you? Wait, listen, don't rush. And then there is the rational mind, the adult mind, which may say something entirely different.

There's no need for your adult mind to agree with your parents. Your parents were not omniscient, they were not all-knowing. They were human beings as fallible as you are, and many times you find loopholes in their thinking. Many times you find them dogmatic, superstitious, believing in foolish things, holding irrational ideologies. Your adult says no. Your parent says do it, your adult says it is not worth doing, and your child is pulling you somewhere else. This is the triangle within you.

If you listen to the child, the parent feels angry. So one part feels good—you can eat as much ice cream as you want—but the parent inside feels angry; a part of you starts condemning. Then you start feeling guilty. The same guilt arises as it used to arise when you were a child. You are no longer a child, but the child has not disappeared. It is there; it is your ground floor, your base, your foundation.

If you follow the child, if you follow the feeling, the parent becomes angry and then you start feeling guilt. If you follow the parent, then your child feels that he is being forced into things which he does not want to do. Then your

> *Buddha says right mindfulness is the only virtue there is*

child feels he is being unnecessarily interfered with, unnecessarily trespassed upon. Freedom is lost when you listen to the parent, and your child starts feeling rebellious.

If you listen to the parent, your adult mind says, "What nonsense! These people never knew anything. You know more, you are more in tune with the modern world, you are more contemporary. These ideologies are just dead ideologies, out of date—why are you bothering?" If you listen to your reason then you also feel as if you are betraying your parents. Again guilt arises. What to do? It is almost impossible to find something on which all these three layers agree.

This is human anxiety. No, never do all these three layers agree on any point. There is no agreement ever.

Now there are teachers who believe in the child. They emphasize the child more. For example, Lao Tzu. He says, "The agreement is not going to come. You drop this parental voice, these commandments, these Old Testaments. Drop all 'shoulds' and become a child again." That's what Jesus says. Lao Tzu

and Jesus—their emphasis is to become a child again—because only with the child will you be able to gain your spontaneity, will you again become part of the natural flow, Tao.

Their message is beautiful, but seems to be almost impractical. Sometimes, yes, it has happened—a person has become a child again. But it is so exceptional that it is not possible to think that humanity is ever going to become a child again. It is beautiful like a star...far distant, but out of reach.

Then there are other teachers—Mahavira, Moses, Mohammed, Manu—who say, listen to the parental voice, listen to the moral, what the society says, what you have been taught. Listen and follow it. If you want to be at ease in the world, if you want to be peaceful in the world, listen to the parent. Never go against the parental voice.

That's how the world has followed, more or less. But then one never feels spontaneous, one never feels natural. One always feels confined, caged. And when you don't feel free, you may feel peaceful, but that peacefulness is worthless. Unless peace comes with freedom, you cannot accept it. Unless peace comes with bliss, you cannot accept it. It brings convenience and comfort, but your soul suffers.

Yes, there have been a few people who have achieved through the parental voice, who have attained the truth. But that, too, is very rare. And that world is gone. Maybe in the past, Moses and Manu and Mohammed were useful. They gave commandments to the world: "Do this. Don't do that." They made things simple, very simple. They have not left anything for you to decide; they don't trust that you will be able to decide. They simply give you a ready-made formula—"These are the Ten Commandments to be followed. You do these and all that you hope, all that you desire, will happen as a consequence. Just be obedient."

All the old religions emphasized obedience too much. Disobedience is the only sin—that's what Christianity says. Adam and Eve were expelled from the garden of God because they disobeyed. God had said not to eat the fruit of the tree of knowledge and they disobeyed. That was their only sin. But every child is committing that sin. The father says, 'Don't smoke," but the child tries it. The father says, "Don't go to the movie," but she goes. The story of Adam and Eve is the story of every child. And then condemnation, expulsion....

Obedience is religion for Manu, Mohammed, Moses. But that world has gone, and through it many have not attained. Many became peaceful, good citizens, respectable members of the society, but nothing much.

Then there is the third emphasis on being adult. Confucius, Patanjali, or modern agnostics like Bertrand Russell—the humanists of the world—all emphasize: "Believe only in your own reason." That seems arduous, so much so that one's whole life becomes a conflict. Because you have been brought up by your parents, you have been conditioned by your parents. If you listen only to your reason, you have to deny many things in your being. In fact, your whole mind has to be denied. It is not easy to erase it.

And you were born, as children, without any reason; that, too, is there. Basically you are a feeling being; reason comes very late. It comes when all that has to happen has

happened. Psychologists say a child learns almost seventy-five percent of his whole knowledge by the time he is seven years old. Seventy-five percent of his whole knowledge he has learned by the time he is seven years old, fifty percent by the time he is four years old. This learning happens when you are a child, and reason comes late. It is a late arrival.

It is difficult to live just with reason. People have tried—a Bertrand Russell here and there—but nobody has achieved truth through it, because reason alone is not enough.

All these angles have been chosen and tried, and nothing has worked. Buddha's standpoint is totally different. That's his original contribution to human consciousness. He says not to choose any, he says move in the center of the triangle. Don't choose reason, don't choose the parent, and don't choose the child. Move in the very center of the triangle and remain silent and become mindful. His approach is tremendously meaningful. And then you will be able to have a clear perspective of your being. Out of that

perspective and clarity, let the response come.

We can say it in another way. If you function as a child, that is a childish reaction. Many times you function as a child. Somebody says something and you get hurt, and in a tantrum of anger and temper you lose everything. Later on you feel bad about it—that you lost your image. Everybody thinks you are so sober yet you were so childish, and nothing much was at stake.

Or you follow your parental voice, but later on you think that still you are dominated by your parents. You have not yet become an adult, mature enough to take the reins of your life into your own hands.

Sometimes you follow reason, but then you think that reason is not enough, feeling also is needed. And without feeling, a rational being becomes just the head; he loses contact with the body, he loses contact with life, he becomes disconnected. He functions only as a thinking mechanism. But thinking cannot make you alive; in thinking there is no juice of life. It is a dry thing. Then you hanker for something that can again allow your energies to stream, can again

allow you to be green and alive and young. This goes on and you go on chasing your own tail.

Buddha says these are all reactions and any reaction is bound to be partial—only response is total, and whatsoever is partial is a mistake. That's his definition of error: whatsoever is partial is a mistake. Because your other parts will remain unfulfilled and they will take their revenge. Be total. Response is total; reaction is partial.

When you listen to one voice and follow it you are getting into trouble. You will never be satisfied with it. Only one part will be satisfied; the other two parts will be dissatisfied. So two-thirds of your being will be dissatisfied, one-third of your being will be satisfied, and you will always remain in a turmoil. Whatsoever you do, reaction can never satisfy you because reaction is partial.

Respond—response is total. Then you don't function from any point on the triangle, you don't choose; you simply remain in a choiceless awareness. You remain centered. And out of that centering you act, whatsoever it is. It is neither child nor parent nor adult. You have gone beyond "PAC." It is you now—your being. That PAC is like a cyclone and your center is the center of the cyclone.

Whenever there is a need to respond, the first thing, Buddha says, is to become mindful, become aware. Remember your center. Become grounded in your center. Be there for a few moments before you do anything.

There is no need to think about it because thinking is partial. There is no need to feel about it because feeling is partial. There is no need to find clues from your parents, the Bible, Koran, Gita—these are all "P'—there is no need. Simply remain tranquil, silent, alert—watching the situation as if you are absolutely out of it, aloof, a watcher on the hills.

This is the first requirement—to be centered whenever you want to act. Then out of this centering let the act arise, and whatsoever you do will be virtuous, whatsoever you do will be right.

Buddha says right mindfulness is the only virtue there is. Not to be mindful is to fall into error. To act unconsciously is to fall into error.

WAIT FOR CLARITY

One day Buddha is passing through a forest. It is a hot summer day and he is feeling very thirsty. He says to Ananda, his caretaker, "Ananda, you go back. Just three, four miles back we passed a small stream of water. You bring a little water—take my begging bowl. I am feeling very thirsty and tired."

Ananda goes back, but by the time he reaches the stream, a few bullock carts have just passed through the stream and they have made the whole stream muddy. Dead leaves that had settled into the bed have risen up; it is no longer possible to drink this water—it is too dirty. He comes back empty-handed, and he says, "You will have to wait a little. I will go ahead. I have heard that just two, three miles ahead there is a big river. I will bring water from there."

But Buddha insists. He says, "You go back and bring water from the same stream."

Ananda could not understand the insistence, but if the master says so, the disciple has to follow. Seeing the absurdity of it—that again he will have to walk three, four miles, and he knows that water is not worth drinking—he goes.

When he is going, Buddha says, "And don't come back if the water is still dirty. If it is dirty, simply sit on the bank silently. Don't do anything, don't get into the stream. Sit on the bank silently and watch. Sooner or later the water will be clear again, and then you fill the bowl and come back."

Ananda goes there. Buddha is right: the water is almost clear, the leaves have moved, the dust has settled. But it is not absolutely clear yet, so he sits on the bank just watching the river flow by. Slowly, slowly, it becomes crystal-clear. Then he comes back dancing; he understands why Buddha was so insistent. There was a certain message in it for him, and he has understood the message. He gives the water to Buddha, and he thanks Buddha, touches his feet.

Buddha says, "What are you doing? I should thank you because you have brought water for me."

Ananda says, "Now I can understand. First I was angry; I didn't show it, but I was angry because it was absurd to go back. But now I understand the message. This is what I actually needed in this moment. The same is the case with my mind—sitting on the bank of that small stream, I became aware that the same is the case with my mind. If I jump into the stream I will make it dirty again. If I jump into the mind more noise is created, more problems start coming up, surfacing. Sitting by the side of the stream, I learned the technique.

"Now I will be sitting by the side of my mind too, watching it with all its dirtiness and problems and old leaves and hurts and wounds, memories, desires. Unconcerned I will sit on the bank and wait for the moment when everything is clear."

via negativa

THE WAY OF the Buddha is known as *via negativa*—the path of negation. This attitude, this approach has to be understood.

Buddha's approach is unique. All other religions of the world are positive religions, they have a positive goal—call it God, liberation, salvation, self-realization—but there is a goal to be achieved. And positive effort is needed on the part of the seeker. Unless you make hard effort you will not reach the goal.

Buddha's approach is totally different, diametrically opposite. He says you are already that which you want to become, the goal is within you; it is your own nature. You are not to achieve it. It is not in the future, it is not somewhere else. It is you right now, this very moment. But there are a few obstacles and those obstacles have to be removed.

It is not that you have to attain godhood—godhood is your nature—but there are a few obstacles to be removed. Once those obstacles are removed, you are that which you have always been seeking. Even when you were not aware of who you are, you were that. You cannot be otherwise. Obstacles have to be eliminated, dropped. Nothing else has to be added to you.

The positive religion tries to add something to you: virtue, righteousness, meditation, prayer. The positive religion says you are lacking something; you have to be in search of that which you are lacking. You have to accumulate something.

Buddha's negative approach says you are not lacking anything. In fact, you are possessing too many things which are not needed. You have to drop something.

It is like this: You go trekking into the Himalayas. The higher you start reaching, the more you will feel the weight of the things you are carrying with you. Your luggage will become more and more heavy. The higher the altitude, the heavier your luggage will become. You will have to drop things. If you want to reach to the highest peak, you will have to drop all.

Once you have dropped all, once you don't possess anything, once you have become a zero, a nothingness, a nobody, you have reached the peak. Something has to be eliminated, not added to you. Something has to be dropped, not accumulated.

When Buddha attained, somebody asked him, "What have you attained?" He laughed. He said, "I have not attained anything, because whatsoever I have attained was always with me. On the contrary, I have lost many things. I have lost my ego. I have lost my thoughts, my mind. I have lost all that I used to feel I possessed. I have lost my body—I used to think I *was* the body. I have lost all that. Now I exist as pure nothingness. This is my achievement."

Let me explain it to you, because this is central.

According to Buddha's approach, in the beginningless beginning of existence there was absolute sleep; existence was fast asleep, snoring, what Hindus call *sushupti*, a state of dreamless sleep. The whole of existence was asleep in sushupti. Nothing was moving, everything was at rest—so tremendously, so utterly at rest, you can say it was not existing at all.

When you move into sushupti every night, when dreams stop, you again move into that primordial nothingness. And if in the night there are not a few moments of that primordial nothingness, you don't feel rejuvenated, you don't feel revitalized. If the whole night you dream, and turn and toss in the bed, in the morning you are more tired than you were when you went to bed. You could not dissolve, you could not lose yourself.

If you have been in *sushupti*, in a dreamless state, that means you moved into that beginningless beginning again. From there is energy. From there you come back rested, vitalized, new. Again full of juice, full of life and zest. That, Buddha says, was the beginning; but he calls it the beginningless beginning. It was like sushupti it was tremendously unconscious; there was no consciousness in it. It was just like *samadhi* enlightenment, with only one difference: in samadhi one is fully awake. In that *sushupti* in that dreamless deep sleep, there was no consciousness, not even a single flame of consciousness—a dark night. It is also a state of utter blissfulness, but the state is unconscious.

In the morning when you become awake, then you say, "Last night was beautiful,

I slept very deeply. It was so beautiful and so full of bliss." But this you say in the morning. When you were really in that sleep, you were not aware; you were absolutely unconscious. When you awake in the morning, then you look retrospectively backward and then you are able to recognize that: "Yes, it was beautiful!"

When a person awakes in *samadhi*, then he recognizes that: "All my lives of the past were all blissful. I have been in a tremendously enchanted, magic world. I have never been miserable." *Then* one recognizes, but right now you cannot recognize—you are unconscious. The primordial state is full of bliss but there is nobody to recognize it. Trees still exist in that primordial state; mountains and the ocean and the clouds and the deserts still exist in that primordial consciousness. It is a state of unconsciousness.

This, Buddha calls nothingness, pure nothingness, because there was no distinction, no demarcation. It was nebulous: no form, no name. It was like a dark night.

Then came the explosion. Scientists also talk about this explosion; they call it the Big Bang. Then everything exploded.

The nothingness disappeared and things appeared. It is still a hypothesis, even for scientists, because nobody can go back. For scientists it is a hypothesis, the most probable hypothesis at most.

There are many theories proposed, propounded, but the Big Bang theory is generally accepted—that out of that nothingness, things exploded like a seed explodes and becomes a tree. And in the tree are millions of seeds, and then they explode. A single seed can fill the earth with greenery. This is what explosion means.

Have you observed the fact? Such mystery! A small seed, barely visible, can explode and fill the whole earth with forests. Not only the whole earth, but all the earths possible in existence. A single seed! And if you break the seed, what will you find inside it? Nothingness, just pure nothing. Out of this nothingness, the whole has evolved.

For scientists it is just a hypothesis, an inference. For a Buddha it is not a hypothesis—it is his experience. He has known this happening within himself.

I will try to explain it to you, how one comes to know this beginningless beginning—because you cannot go back, but there is a way to move ahead. And, just as everything moves in a circle, time also moves in a circle.

In the West, the concept of time is linear; time moves in a line, horizontal; it goes on and on and on. But in the East, we believe in a circular time, and the Eastern concept of time is closer to reality, because every movement is circular. The earth moves in a circle, the moon moves in a circle, the stars move in a circle. The year moves in a circle, *life* moves in a circle: birth, childhood, youth, old age—again birth! What you call death is again birth. Again childhood, again youth...and the wheel goes on moving. The year goes round and round:

summer comes, and the rains, and the winter and again summer. Everything is moving in a circle. Why should there be an exception for time? Time also moves in a circle. One cannot go backward but if you go on ahead, moving ahead, one day, time starts moving in a circle. You reach the beginningless beginning or, now you can call it, the endless end.

Buddha has known it, experienced it.

What the scientists call the Big Bang, I call cosmic orgasm. That seems to me more meaningful. "Big Bang" looks a little ugly, too technological, inhuman. Cosmic orgasm— the cosmos exploded into orgasm. Millions of forms were born out of it. And it was a tremendously blissful experience, so let us call it cosmic orgasm.

In that orgasm three things developed. First, the universe, what we in the East call *sat*. Out of the universe developed life, what we call *ananda*. And out of life developed mind, what we call *chit*. *Sat* means being; *ananda* means celebrating the being—when a tree comes to bloom, it is celebrating its being. And *chit* means consciousness—when you have become conscious about your bliss, about your celebration. These three states: *satchitananda*.

Humanity has come up to the mind. The rocks are still at the first stage, the universe— they exist but they don't flower, they don't celebrate. They are closed, coiled upon themselves. Some day they will start moving, some day they will open their petals, but right now they are caved within themselves, completely closed.

Trees and animals have come to the next stage, life—so happy, so beautiful, so colorful.

The birds go on singing, and the trees go on blooming. This is the second stage, life. The third stage, only humans have reached: the state of mind, the state of *chit*—consciousness.

Buddha says these three are like a dream. The first, the beginningless beginning, the primordial state, is like sleep—*sushupti*. These three are like a drama that is unfolding. If you move beyond mind, if you start moving toward meditation, that is, toward no-mind, again another explosion happens. But now it is no longer an explosion, it is implosion. Just as one day the explosion happened and millions of things were born out of nothingness, so when implosion happens, forms and names disappear—again nothingness is born out of it. The circle is complete.

Scientists talk only about explosion, they don't talk about implosion yet, which is illogical. Because if explosion is possible, then implosion is also possible.

A seed is thrown into the earth. It explodes. A tree is born, then on the tree again seeds are born. What is a seed now? When the seed explodes, it is a tree. When the tree implodes, it is again a seed. The seed was carrying a tree; it opened itself and became a tree. Now the tree again closes itself, caves in, becomes a small seed.

If explosion happened in the world, as scientists now trust, then the Buddhist idea of implosion is also a reality. Explosion cannot exist without implosion. They go together. Implosion means that again mind moves into life, life moves into universe, universe moves into nothingness and the circle is complete. Nothingness moves into universe, universe moves into life, life moves into mind, mind again moves into life, life again into universe, universe again into nothingness... the circle is complete.

After implosion, when it has happened, when everything has again come to nothingness, there is a difference. The first nothingness was unconscious; this second nothingness is conscious. The first was like darkness, the second is like light. The first was like night, the second is like day. The first we called *sushupti*; the second we will call *jagriti*—awareness, fully awake. This is the whole circle.

The first, scientists call the Big Bang theory because there was so much explosion and so much noise. It *was* a big bang. A moment

> *Religion means becoming conscious of that which you are*

before, everything was silent, there was no noise, no sound, and after one moment, when existence exploded, there was so much sound and so much noise. All sorts of noises started.

What happens when the explosion disappears into an implosion? The soundless sound. Now there is no longer any noise. Again everything is silent. This is what Zen calls the sound of one hand clapping. This is what Hindus have called *anahatnada*, *omkar*—the soundless sound.

The first, Hindus have called *nadavisphot*—big bang, the sound exploded. And the second is when the sound again moves into silence; the story is complete. Science is still clinging to the half story; the other half is missing. And one who watches this whole play—from sushupti, the dark night of the soul, to dream, and from dream to awareness—the one who watches it all is the witness. The fourth state we call *turiya*—the one who witnesses all. That one known, you become a buddha; that one known, experienced, you have attained.

But the point to be understood is this: that all the time, when you are asleep or dreaming or awake, you are that. Sometimes not aware, sometimes aware, that is the only difference—your nature remains the same.

T.S. Eliot has written a few beautiful lines:

We shall not cease from exploration
and the end of all our exploring
will be to arrive where we started
and know the place for the first time.

This is the meaning of Buddha's renunciation, his path of *via negativa*. You have to come to the point from where you started. You have to know that which you already are. You have to achieve that which is already achieved. You have to achieve that which, in the nature of things, cannot be lost; there is no way to lose contact with it. At the most we can become unconscious about it.

Religion means becoming conscious of that which you are. It is not a search for something new; it is an effort to know that which has always been there, is eternal. From the beginningless beginning to the endless end, it is always there.

Because the path is negative, there are a few difficulties about it. It is difficult to be attracted to Buddhism, because ordinarily the mind wants something positive to cling to, the mind wants something to achieve—and Buddha says there is nothing to achieve; rather, on the contrary, you have to lose something.

Just the idea of losing something is unappealing, because our social concept is of having more and more and more. Buddha says *having* is the problem. The more you have, the less you are; because the more you have, the less you can recognize yourself—you are lost.

Your emptiness, your space is covered too much by things. A rich man is poor—poor because he has no space left, poor because everything is occupied, poor because he does not know any emptiness in his being. Through emptiness you have the glimpses of the primordial and the ultimate—and they are both the same.

It is difficult to be attracted to Buddhism. Only rare people who have a quality of tremendous intelligence can be attracted to it. It cannot become a mass religion. When it became a mass religion it became so only when it lost all its originality, when it compromised with the masses.

In India Buddhism disappeared because the followers of Buddha insisted on its purity. There are people who think that it is because Hindu philosophers and Hindu mystics refuted Buddhism, that's why Buddhism disappeared from India—that is wrong. It cannot be refuted. Nobody has ever refuted it. There is no possibility of refuting it because in the first place it's not based on logic.

If something is based on logic, you can destroy it by logic. If something is based on logical proof, you can refute it. Buddhism is not based on logic at all. It is based on experience; it is existential. It does not believe in any metaphysics—how can you refute it? It never asserts anything about any concept. It simply describes the innermost experience. It has no philosophy, so philosophers cannot refute it.

But it is true that Buddhism disappeared from India. The basic cause of its disappearance is that Buddha and his followers insisted on its

purity. The very insistence on its purity became an unbridgeable gap. The masses could not understand it—only rare people, a very cultured, intelligent, aristocratic few, a chosen few could understand what Buddha meant. Those who understood it, in their very understanding were transformed. But for the masses it was meaningless. It lost its hold on the masses.

In China it succeeded. In Tibet, in Ceylon, in Burma, in Thailand, in Japan, it succeeded—because the missionaries, the Buddhist missionaries who went out of India, seeing what had happened in India, became very

compromising. They compromised.
They started talking in the positive language.
They started talking about achievement, bliss,
heaven—from the back door they brought
in everything that Buddha had denied. Again
the masses were happy. The whole of China,
the whole of Asia was converted to Buddhism—
except India. In India they tried to give only the
pure message, without any compromise; that
was not possible. In China, Buddhism became
a mass religion, but then it lost its truth.

Let me tell you one anecdote:

*A junior devil has been sent to earth to
look around and see how things are
progressing. He quickly returns to hell,
horrified, and obtains an interview with
Beelzebub, the chief devil himself.*

*"Sir," he sputters, "something awful has
happened! There is a man with a beard walking
around on earth, speaking truth, and people are
beginning to listen to him. Something has to be
done immediately."*

*Beelzebub smiles pleasantly, puffing on his
pipe but making no comment.*

*"Sir! You don't realize the seriousness of the
situation," continues the distraught junior devil.
"Pretty soon all will be lost!"*

*Beelzebub removes his pipe slowly, taps it
out on the ashtray, and sits back in his swivel
chair, hands behind his head.*

*"Don't worry, son," he counsels. "We will let
it go on a little longer and, when it has
progressed far enough, we will step in and help
them to organize!"*

Once a religion is organized, it is dead—
because you can organize a religion only when
you compromise with the masses. You can
organize a religion only when you follow the
desires of the common mass. You can organize
a religion only when you are ready to make it
politics and you are ready to lose its religiousness.

A religion can be organized only when it is
no longer a real religion. That is to say, a religion
cannot be organized as *religion*. Organized,
it is no longer religion. A real religion basically
remains unorganized, remains a little chaotic,
remains a little disorderly—because real religion
is freedom.

the religionless religion

THE WAY OF THE Buddha is not a religion in the ordinary sense of the term, because it has no belief system, no dogma, no scripture. It does not believe in God, it does not believe in the soul, it does not

believe in any paradise. It is a tremendous unbelief—and yet it is a religion. It is unique. Nothing has ever happened like it before in the history of human consciousness, and nothing afterward.

Buddha remains utterly unique, incomparable. He says that God is nothing but a search for security, a search for safety, a search for shelter. You believe in God, not because God is there; you believe in God because you feel helpless without that belief. Even if there is no God, you will invent one. The temptation comes from your weakness. It is a projection.

Humans feel limited, helpless, almost victims of circumstance—not knowing from where they come, not knowing where they are going, not knowing why they are here. If there is no God it is difficult for ordinary people to have any meaning in life. The ordinary mind will go berserk without God. God is a prop—it helps you, it consoles you, it comforts you. It says, "Don't be worried—the Almighty God knows everything about why you are here. He is the Creator, He knows why He has created the world. You may not know but the Father knows, and you can trust in Him." It is a great consolation.

The very idea of God gives you a sense of relief—that you are not alone; that somebody is looking after the affairs; that this cosmos is not just chaos, it is truly a cosmos; that there is a system behind it; that there is logic behind it; it is not an illogical jumble of things; it is not anarchy. Somebody rules the cosmos; the sovereign King is there looking after each small detail—not even a leaf moves without His moving it. Everything is planned. You are part of a great destiny. Maybe the meaning is not known to you, but the meaning is there because God is there.

God brings a tremendous relief. One can believe that life is not accidental; there is a certain undercurrent of significance, meaning, destiny. God brings a sense of destiny.

Buddha says there is no God—it simply shows that we do not know why we are here. It shows our helplessness. It shows that there is no meaning available to us. By creating the idea of God we can believe in meaning, and we can live this futile life with the idea that somebody is looking after it.

Just think: you are in an airplane and somebody says, "There is no pilot." Suddenly there will be a panic. No pilot?! No pilot means you are doomed. Then somebody says, "The pilot is there, but invisible. We may not be able to see the pilot, but he is there; otherwise, how is this beautiful mechanism functioning? Just think of it: everything is going so beautifully, there must be a pilot! Maybe we are not capable of seeing him, maybe we are not yet prayerful enough to see him, maybe our eyes are closed, but the pilot is there. Otherwise, how is it possible? This airplane has taken off, it is flying perfectly well, the engines are humming. Everything is a proof that there is a pilot."

If somebody proves it, you relax again into your chair. You close your eyes, you start dreaming again, you can fall asleep. The pilot is there; you need not worry.

Buddha says: The pilot exists not; it is a human creation. Humankind has created God in its own image. It is a human invention—God is not a discovery, it is an invention. And God is not the truth, it is the greatest lie there is.

That's why I say Buddhism is not a religion in the ordinary sense of the term. A Godless religion—can you imagine? When for the first time Western scholars became aware of Buddhism, they were shocked. They could not comprehend that a religion can exist and be without God. They had known only Judaism, Christianity, and Islam. All these three religions are in a way very immature compared with Buddhism.

Buddhism is religion come of age. Buddhism is the religion of a mature mind. Buddhism is not childish at all, and it doesn't support any childish desires in you. It is merciless. Let me repeat it: There has never been a man more compassionate than Buddha, but his religion is merciless.

In fact, in that mercilessness he is showing his compassion. He will not allow you to cling to any lie. Howsoever consoling, a lie is a lie. Those who have given you the lie are not friends to you, they are enemies—because under the impact of the lie you will live a life full of lies. The truth has to be brought to you, howsoever hard, howsoever shattering, howsoever shocking. Even if you are annihilated by the impact of the truth, it is good.

Buddha says: The truth is that human religions are human inventions. You are in a dark night surrounded by alien forces. You need someone to hang on to, someone to cling to. And everything that you can see is changing—your father will die one day and you will be left alone, your mother will die one day and you will be left alone, and you will be an orphan. From childhood you have been accustomed to having a father to protect you, a mother to love you. Now that childish desire will again assert itself: you will need a father figure. If you cannot find it in the sky, then you will find it in some politician.

Stalin became the father of Soviet Russia; they had dropped the idea of God. Mao became the father of China; they had dropped the idea of God. But people are such that they cannot live without a father figure. People are childish! There are very few rare people who grow to be mature.

My own observation is this: people remain near the age of seven, eight, or nine. Their physical bodies go on growing but their minds remain stuck somewhere below the age of ten. Christianity, Judaism, Islam, Hinduism, are religions below the age of ten. They fulfill whatever are your needs; they are not too concerned with the truth. They are more concerned with you, concerned about how to console you.

Don't hide behind beliefs and masks and theologies. Take hold of your life in your own hands

The situation is such: the mother has died and the child is crying and weeping, and you have to console the child. So you tell lies. You pretend that the mother has not died: "She has gone for a visit to the neighbors—she will be coming. Don't be worried, she will be coming right back." Or, "She has gone for a long journey. It will take a few days but she will be back." Or, "She has gone to visit God—nothing to be worried about. She is still alive—maybe she has left the body, but the soul lives forever."

Buddha is the most shattering individual in the history of humanity. His whole effort is to drop all props. He does not say to believe in anything. He is an unbeliever and his religion is that of unbelief. He does not say "believe," he says "doubt."

Now, you have heard about religions that say "Believe!" You have never heard about a religion that says "Doubt!" Doubt is the very methodology—doubt to the very core, doubt to the very end, doubt to the very last. When you have doubted everything, and you have dropped everything through doubt, then reality arises in your vision. It has nothing to do with your beliefs about God. It is nothing like your so-called God. Then arises reality, absolutely unfamiliar and unknown.

But that possibility exists only when all beliefs have been dropped and the mind has come to a state of maturity, understanding, and acceptance that "Whatsoever is, is, and we don't desire otherwise. If there is no God, there is no God, and we don't have any desire to project a God. If there is no God, then we accept it." This is what maturity is: to accept the fact and not to create a fiction around it; to accept the reality as it is, without trying to sweeten it, without trying to decorate it, without trying to make it more acceptable to your heart. If it is shattering, it is shattering. If it is shocking, it is shocking. If the truth kills, then one is ready to be killed.

Buddha is merciless. And nobody has ever opened the door of reality so deeply, so profoundly as he has done. He does not allow you any childish desires. He says: Become more aware, become more conscious, become more courageous. Don't hide behind beliefs and masks and theologies. Take hold of your life in your own hands. Burn bright your inner light and see whatsoever is. And once you have become courageous enough to accept it, it is a benediction. No belief is needed.

That is Buddha's first step towards reality, to say that all belief systems are poisonous; all belief systems are barriers.

He is not a theist. And remember he is not an atheist, either—because, as he says, a few people believe that there is God and a few people believe that there is no God, but both are believers. His nonbelief is so deep that even those who say there is no God, and believe in it, are not acceptable to him. He says that just to say there is no God makes no difference. If you remain childish, you will create another source of God.

For example, Karl Marx declared there was no God, but then he created a God out of history. History becomes the God; the same function is being done now by history that was done previously by the concept of God. What was God doing? God was the determining factor; God was the managing factor. It was God

who was deciding what should be and what should not be. Marx dropped the idea of God, but then history became the determining factor. Then history became the fate, then history became *kismet*—then history is determining everything. Now, what is history? Marx says communism is an inevitable state. History has determined that it will come, and everything is determined by history. Now history becomes a super-God.

But somebody or something to determine reality is needed. People cannot live with indeterminate reality. People cannot live with reality as it is—chaotic, accidental. People cannot live with reality without finding some idea which makes it meaningful, relevant, continuous, which gives it a shape that reason can understand; which can be dissected, analyzed into cause and effect.

Freud dropped the idea of God, but then the unconscious became the God—then everything is determined by the unconscious, and people are helpless in the hands of the unconscious. These are new names for God; it is a new mythology. The Freudian psychology is a new mythology about God. The name is changed but the content remains the same. The label has changed, the old label has been dropped and a fresh, newly painted label has been put on it—it can deceive people who are not very alert. But if you go deeper into Freudian analysis you will immediately see that the unconscious is doing the same work that God used to do.

So what is wrong with poor God? If you have to invent something—and one has always to be determined by something...history, economics, the unconscious, this and that—if

one cannot be free, then what is the point of changing mythologies, theologies? It makes not much difference. You may be a Hindu, you may be a Mohammedan, you may be a Christian, you may be a Jew—it makes not much difference. Your mind remains childish, you remain immature. You remain in search, you continue to search for a father figure—someone, somewhere, who can explain everything, who can become the ultimate explanation. The mature mind is one who can remain without any search even if there is no ultimate explanation of things.

That's why Buddha says, "I am not a metaphysician." He has no metaphysics. Metaphysics means the ultimate explanation about things, and he has no ultimate explanation. He does not say, "I have solved the mystery." He does not say, "Here, I hand over to you what truth is." He says, "The only thing that I can give to you is an impetus, a thirst, a tremendous passion to become aware, to become conscious, to become alert; to live your life so consciously, so full of light and awareness, that *your life* is solved."

Not that you come to some ultimate explanation of existence—nobody ever has. Buddha denies metaphysics completely. He says metaphysics is a futile search.

The first thing is that he denies God.

The second thing is that he denies paradise, heaven. He says: Your heaven, your paradise, are nothing but your unfulfilled sexual desires, unfulfilled instincts being projected into the other life, the life beyond, the life after death. And he seems to be absolutely right. If you see the descriptions of heaven and paradise in

Islam, in Christianity, in Judaism, you will understand perfectly what he is saying. Whatever remains unfulfilled here, you go on projecting in the hereafter. But the desire seems to be the same!

Hindus say there are trees they call *kalpvraksha*—you sit under them and whatsoever you desire, without any lapse of time, is fulfilled. You desire a beautiful woman, she is there—immediately, instantly. In the West you have invented instant coffee and things like that just recently. India discovered a wish-fulfilling tree, and down the centuries has believed in it. The tree is instantly fulfilling—truly instantly, without any time lapse. Here the idea arises, there it is fulfilled; not a single second passes between the two. The idea *is* its fulfillment—you desire a beautiful woman, she is there. You desire delicious food, it is there. You desire a comfortable bed to rest on, it is there.

Now, this is simple psychological analysis. That man is unfulfilled in life, and he spends his whole life trying to fulfill it—still he finds it cannot be fulfilled, so he has to project his desires into the future. Not that in the future they can be fulfilled—desire as such is unfulfillable.

Buddha has said: The very nature of desire is that it remains unfulfilled. Whatever you do, regardless of what you do about it, it remains unfulfilled—that is the intrinsic nature of desire. *Desire as such* remains unfulfilled. So you can sit under a wish-fulfilling tree, it won't make any difference. You can feel many times that your desire is being fulfilled, and again it arises. Ad infinitum it will go on arising again and again and again.

The Christian, the Muslim, the Jew, the Hindu—all heavens and paradises are nothing but unfulfilled projected desires, repressed desires, frustrated desires. Of course, they console man very much: "If you have not been able to fulfill them here—there. Sooner or later you will reach God; the only thing you have to do is go on praying to him, go on bowing down before some image or some idea or some ideal, and keep him happy. Keep God happy, and then you will reap a great crop of pleasures and gratifications. That will be God's gift to you for your prayers, for your appreciation, for continuous surrender, for again and again touching his feet, for your obedience—that is going to be the reward."

The reward is, of course, after death, because even cunning priests cannot deceive you in this life—even they cannot deceive. They know that desire remains unfulfilled, so they have to invent an afterlife. Nobody has known the afterlife but people can be deceived very easily. If somebody comes and says to you, "God can fulfill your desire here and now," it will be difficult to prove it—because nobody's desire has ever been fulfilled here and now. Then their God will be at stake. They have invented a very cunning device; they say, "After this life...."

Is your God not potent enough to fulfill your desires here? Is your God not potent enough to create wish-fulfillment trees on the earth? Is your God not powerful enough to do something while people are alive? If he cannot fulfill anything here, what is the proof that he is going to fulfill anything hereafter?

Buddha says: Look into the nature of desire. Watch the movement of desire; it is very subtle. And you will be able to see two things: one, that desire by its very nature is unfulfillable. And second, the moment you understand that desire is unfulfillable, desire disappears and you are left desireless. That is the state of peace, silence, tranquility. That is the state of fulfillment! People never come to fulfillment through desire; they come to fulfillment only by transcending desire.

Desire is a great opportunity to understand the functioning of your own mind—how it functions, what the mechanism of it is. And when you have understood that, in that very understanding is transformation. Desire disappears, leaves no trace behind. And when you are desireless, not desiring anything, you are fulfilled. Not that desire is fulfilled, but when desire is transcended there is fulfillment.

Now see the difference. Other religions say, "Desires can be fulfilled in the other world." The worldly people say, "Desires can be fulfilled here." The communists say, "Desires can be fulfilled here. Just a different social structure is needed, just the capitalists have to be overthrown, the proletariat has to take over, the bourgeoisie has to be destroyed, that's all—and desires can be fulfilled here, heaven can be created on this earth here."

The worldly people say, "You can fulfill your desires—struggle hard." That's what the West is doing: "Struggle, compete, succeed by any means and methods. Acquire more wealth, more power!" That's what politicians all over the world are doing: "Become more powerful and your desires can be fulfilled." That's what scientists say, that only a few more technologies have to be invented and paradise is just around the corner. And what do your religions say? They don't say anything different. They say, "Desires can be fulfilled, but not in this life—after death." That is the only difference between the so-called materialists and so-called religious.

To Buddha, both are materialists; and to me also, both are materialists. Your so-called religious people and your so-called irreligious people are both in the same boat. Not a bit of difference! Their attitudes are the same, their approaches are the same.

> *Desire cannot be fulfilled because its nature is to remain unfulfilled and projected in the future*

Buddha is religious in this way, that he says: *Desire cannot be fulfilled*. You have to look into desire. Neither here nor anywhere else has desire ever been fulfilled—never. It has never happened and never is it going to happen because it is against the nature of desire. What is desire? Have you ever looked into your desiring mind? Have you encountered it? Have you tried any meditation on it? What is desire?

You desire a certain house; you work for it, you work hard. You destroy your whole life for it—then the house is there. But is fulfillment there? Once the house is there, suddenly you feel empty—you feel more empty than before, because before there was an occupation to achieve this house. Now that it is there, immediately your mind starts looking for something else to occupy it. Now there are bigger houses; your mind starts thinking of those bigger houses. There are bigger palaces.... You desire a partner and you have achieved your desire, then suddenly your hands are again empty. Again you start desiring some other lover. This is the nature of desire. Desire always goes ahead of you. Desire is always in the future.

Desire is a hope. Desire cannot be fulfilled because its nature is to remain unfulfilled and projected in the future. It is always on the horizon. You can rush, you can run toward the horizon, but you will never reach it: wherever you go you will find the horizon has receded and the distance between you and the horizon remains absolutely the same. You have ten thousand dollars, your desire is for twenty thousand dollars; you have twenty thousand dollars, your desire is for forty thousand dollars. The distance is the same; the mathematical proportion is the same.

Whatever you have, desire always stays ahead of it.

Buddha says: *Abandon hope, abandon desire*. In abandoning hope, in abandoning desire, you will be here now. Without desire, you will be fulfilled. It is desire that is deceiving you.

So when Buddha said that these so-called religious people are all materialists, of course the Hindus were angry—very angry; they had never been so angry against anybody. They tried to uproot Buddha's religion from India, and they succeeded. Buddhism was born in India but Buddhism doesn't exist now in India, because the religion of the Hindus is one of the most materialistic religions in the world. Just look in the Vedas: all prayer, all worship is just asking for more, for more, from gods or from God—all sacrifice is for more. All worship is desire oriented. "Give us more! Give us plenty! Better crops, better rain, more money, more health, more life, more longevity—give us more!" The Veda is nothing but desire written large, and sometimes ugly. In the Veda not only do the sages pray "Give us more!"—they also pray: "Don't give to our enemies! Give more milk to my cow, but let the enemy's cow die, or let its milk disappear."

What type of religion is this? Even to call it religion looks absurd. If this is religion, then what is materialism? Buddha himself had gone to many masters while he was searching, but from everywhere he came back empty-handed—because he could not see that anybody had understood the nature of desire. They themselves were desiring; of course, their desire was projected in the faraway future, the other life, but still the object of desire was the same, the desiring mind was the same. It is only a question of time.

A few people desire things for before their death, a few people desire things for after their death, but what is the difference? There is no difference. They desire the same things—they desire! The desire is the same.

Buddha went to many teachers and was frustrated. He could not see religion flowering anywhere, blossoming—they were all materialistic people. They were great ascetics: somebody was fasting for months, somebody was standing for months, somebody had not slept for years, and they were just skeletons. You could not call them worldly and materialistic if you looked at their bodies... but look at their minds, ask them, "Why are you fasting? Why are you trying so hard? For what?" and there surfaces the desire—to attain to paradise, to heaven, to have eternal gratification in the afterlife.

Listen to their logic and they all will say, "Here, things are fleeting. This life is temporary.

Even if you attain everything is taken away when you die, so what is the point? This life is not going to be forever. We are searching for something that will remain forever—we are after immortality, we are after *absolute* gratification. People who are running after desires here in this life are fools, because death will take everything away. You accumulate wealth and here comes death and all is left behind. We are searching for some treasure that we can take with ourselves, that will never be lost, that cannot be stolen, no government can tax it—nobody can take it away, not even death."

You call these people religious people? They seem to be even worldlier than the so-called worldly; they are more materialistic than the materialists. Of course, their materialism is garbed in a disguise; their materialism has a flavor of spirituality—but it is a deception.

> *Buddha is down-to-earth. He never flies high into metaphysics*

Koran descended on Mohammed from heaven above.

Why do these religions insist that their scriptures, and especially only *their* scriptures, not anybody else's? Mohammedans are not ready to accept that the Vedas are God-made, neither are Hindus ready to accept that the Koran is God-made—only their Vedas are God-made and everything else is just manufactured. Why this insistence? Because they are aware that whatever people create will have the imprint of human mind and human desires.

Buddha says all the scriptures are man-made, and he is right. He is not a fanatic at all. He does not belong to any country and he does not belong to any race; he does not belong to any religion, to any sect. He is simply a light unto himself. And whatsoever he has said is the purest statement of truth ever made.

A friend sent me this beautiful anecdote:

One of the religious leaders in Ireland was asked by his followers to select a suitable burial place and monument for his mortal remains. A religious war was in progress and his life had

been threatened. Three separate plans had been submitted to him, and to the dismay of the committee he chose the least expensive. He was asked why he had made this selection, why he had chosen this humble resting-place when the other two designs were of magnificent tombs.

"Well, my dear friends," he told them, "I appreciate your generosity. But is it worth all this expense when I don't expect to remain in my tomb for more than three days?"

Now, this sort of dogmatic certainty you will never find in Buddha. He is very hesitant. There is only one other name that is also so hesitant and he is Lao Tzu; these two persons are hesitant.

Sometimes, because of their hesitance, they may not impress you—because you are confused, you need somebody to be so confident that you can rely on him. Hence, fanatics impress you.

They may not have anything to say, but they beat the table so much, they make such a fuss about it that their fuss itself gives you the feeling that they must know, otherwise how can they be so certain? Some religious sects are so dogmatic in their assertions that they create a feeling of certainty. And confused people need certainty.

When you come to a buddha, you may not be immediately impressed because he will be so hesitant, he will not assert anything. He knows better than that. He knows that life cannot be confined to any statement, and all statements are partial. No statement can contain the whole truth, so how can you be certain about it? He will remain always relative.

Two great masters of India, Buddha and Mahavira, both were deep into relativity. Einstein discovered it late; Einstein brought relativity to the world of science. Before Einstein, scientists were certain, dogmatically certain, absolutely certain. Einstein brought relativity and humbleness to science; he brought truth to science.

The same was done by Buddha and Mahavira in India: they brought relativity, the concept that truth cannot be asserted totally, that we can never be certain about it, that at the most we can hint at it. The hint has to be indirect; we cannot pinpoint it directly—it is so big, so vast. And it is natural that we fragile human beings should hesitate. This hesitation shows alertness.

You will always find ignorant people to be dogmatic. The more ignorant a person is, the more dogmatic. This is one of the greatest misfortunes in the world, that the foolish are absolutely certain and the wise are hesitant. Buddha is hesitant.

So if you want to understand him, you will have to be alert and open in your listening. He is not delivering truth to you wholesale. He is simply hinting at it...giving indications at the most, and they, too, are subtle.

As I told you, Buddha is down-to-earth. He never flies high into metaphysics. He never introduces; in fact, he has no preface to his statements. He says them directly, immediately, as simply as possible.

Sometimes his statements do not appear to be of any profound depth—they are. But he does not beat around the bush, he does not make any fuss about it.

I have heard:

She was a sweet young thing; he was a fast-rising account executive with a well-known advertising agency. Everyone thought it was an ideal marriage. But alas, there was a problem....with sex. The honeymoon hadn't even begun. "Being an advertising man," she sobbed to a friend, "all he does every night is sit on the edge of the bed and tell me how wonderful it's going to be!"

But it never happens!

Buddha has no preface. He never advertises what he is going to say. He simply says it and moves on. He says:

Moved by their selfish desires, people seek after fame and glory. But when they have acquired it, they are already stricken in years. If you hanker after worldly fame and practice not the way, your labors are wrongfully applied and your energy is wasted. It is like burning an incense stick. However much its pleasing odor be admired, the fire that consumes is steadily burning up the stick.

A simple and matter-of-fact statement: *Moved by their selfish desires, people seek after fame and glory.*

What is a selfish desire? In the Buddhist way of expression, a selfish desire is one that is based in the self. Ordinarily, in ordinary language we call a desire selfish if it is against somebody else and you don't care about others. Even if it harms others, you go ahead and fulfill your desire. People call you selfish because you don't care for others, you have no consideration for others.

But when Buddha says a desire is selfish, his meaning is different. He says: If a desire is based in the idea of *self* then it is selfish. For example, you donate money—a million dollars for some good cause, for hospitals to be constructed or schools to be opened, or food to be distributed to the poor, or medicine to be sent to poor parts of the country. Nobody will call it a selfish desire.

Buddha will say it is—if there is any motivation of self. If you think that by donating a million dollars you are going to earn some virtue and be rewarded in heaven, it is a selfish desire. It may not be harmful to others—it is not; in fact, everybody will appreciate it. People will call you great, religious, virtuous; a person of charity, love, compassion, sympathy. But Buddha will say the only thing that determines whether a desire is selfish or not is its motivation.

If you have donated without any motivation, then it is not selfish. If there is any motivation hidden somewhere—conscious, unconscious—that you are going to gain something out of it, here or hereafter, then it is a selfish desire. That which comes out of the self is a selfish desire; that which comes as part of the ego is a selfish desire. If you meditate just to attain to your selfhood, then it is a selfish desire.

Buddha has said to his disciples: Whenever you meditate, after each meditation, surrender all that you have earned out of meditation, surrender it to the universe. If you are blissful, pour it back into the universe—don't carry it as a treasure. If you are feeling very happy, share it immediately. Don't become attached to it, otherwise your meditation itself will become a new process of the self. And the ultimate meditation is not a process of the self. The ultimate meditation is a process of getting more and more into un-self, into non-self—it is a disappearance of the self.

Buddha says, *Moved by their selfish desires, people seek after fame and glory. But when they have acquired it, they are already stricken in years.* Look—you can attain fame, glory, power, prestige, respectability in the world. But what are you doing? Are you aware? You are wasting a great opportunity, and for something absolutely meaningless. You are collecting rubbish and destroying your own time, your own life energy.

He says, *If you hanker after worldly fame and practice not the way...* Buddha always calls his religion "the way"—*dhamma*, just "the way."

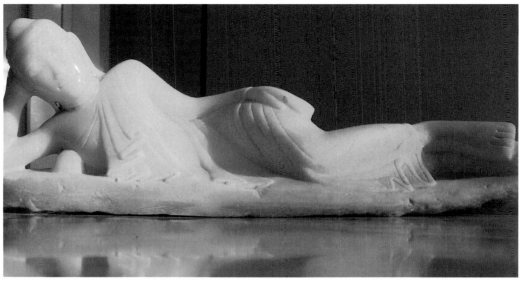

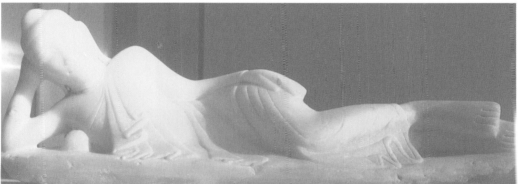

He says, Don't be bothered about the goal; the goal will take care of itself. You simply follow the way, not even with the motivation to reach any goal but out of the sheer delight of meditating, of praying, of loving, of being compassionate, of sharing. Out of sheer delight you practice the way. Not that you are going to gain any profit out of it; don't make it a business.

Life is slipping by; each moment a precious moment is gone and it cannot be reclaimed. Buddha says: Don't waste it in foolish things.

Fame is foolish, it is pointless, meaningless. Even if the whole world knows you, how does it make you richer? How does it make your life

more blissful? How does it help you to be more understanding, to be more aware, to be more alert, to be more alive?

If you are not practicing the way, he says, *Your labors are wrongfully applied and your energy is wasted. It is like burning an incense stick. However much its pleasing odor be admired, the fire that consumes is steadily burning up the stick.*

That's how life is—each moment burning. You are always on the funeral pyre because each moment death is coming closer, each moment you are less alive, more dead. So before this opportunity is lost, Buddha says, attain to a state of no-self. Then there will be no death. Then there will be no misery. And then there will be no constant hankering for fame, power, prestige.

In fact, the more empty you are within, the more you seek fame. It is a sort of substitute. The poorer you are within, the more you seek riches; it is a substitute to fill yourself with something.

I observe it every day: whenever people have a problem with love, they immediately start eating too much. Whenever they feel that their love is in a crisis, they are not being loved, or they are not able to love, something has blocked their love energy, they immediately start stuffing themselves with things. They start eating. Why? What are they doing with the food? They feel empty and that emptiness makes them afraid. They have to somehow stuff it with food.

If you are feeling happy inside, you don't bother about fame; only unhappy people bother about fame. Who bothers whether anybody knows you or not, if you know yourself? If you know yourself, who you are, then there is no need. But when you don't know who you are you would like everybody to know—you want everybody to know who you are. You will collect opinions, you will collect people's ideas, and out of that collection you will try to arrange some identity: "Yes, I am this person. People say to me that I am intelligent, so I must be intelligent." You are not certain. If you were certain, why bother with what people say or don't say?

You look into people's eyes to see your face—you don't know your own face. You beg: "Say something about me. Say I am beautiful. Say I am lovable. Say I am charismatic. Say

something about me!" Have you watched yourself begging? "Say something about my body, about my mind, about my understanding—say something!"

You immediately grab onto it if somebody says something. But if it is shocking and shattering, you become angry. The person is destroying your image if he says something against you. If he says something in favor of you, he helps your image to be a little more decorated, it becomes a little more ornamental, and you come home happy. If people applaud you, you feel happy. Why?

You don't know who you are. That's why you are seeking. You ask people "Who am I? Tell me!" Then you have to depend on them. The irony of it is that those same people don't know who *they* are! Beggars begging from other beggars. They have come to beg from you, so there is a mutual deception.

A man meets a woman and says, "How beautiful! How divine!" And she says, "Yes, and I have never come across such a beautiful man as you." This is a mutual deception. They may call it love, but this is a mutual deception. Both are hankering for a certain identity around themselves. Both fulfill each other's desires. Things will go well until one of the two decides that enough is enough and starts dropping the deception. Then the honeymoon is over...and marriage starts. Then things become ugly. Then he thinks, "This woman deceived me" and she thinks, "This man deceived me." Nobody can deceive you unless you are ready to be deceived, remember. Nobody has ever deceived anybody unless they were ready to be deceived, waiting to be deceived.

You cannot deceive a person who knows himself, because there is no way. If you say something he will laugh. He will say, "Don't be worried about it—I already know who I am. You can drop that subject and go ahead with whatever you have to say. Don't be bothered about me— myself know who I am."

Once you have an inner richness of life, you don't seek wealth, you don't seek power. Psychologists have become aware that when people start becoming impotent, they start seeking sexual, phallic symbols to compensate. If a person becomes impotent then he may try to have the biggest car—that is a phallic symbol.

He would like to have the most powerful car in the world; his own power is lost, his own sexual energy is gone, and he would like a substitute. While pushing his car to the maximum speed, he will feel good—as if he is making love to his woman. The speed will give

> *People cleave to their worldly possessions and selfish passions so blindly as to sacrifice their own lives for them*

him power. He will identify with the car. Psychologists have been watching the phenomenon for many years, that people who have a certain inferiority complex always become ambitious. In fact, almost nobody goes into politics unless he is deeply rooted in an inferiority complex. Politicians are basically people with inferiority complexes. They have to prove their superiority in some way; otherwise, they will not be able to live with their inferiority complex. What I am trying to point out is that whatever you miss within, you try to accumulate something outside as a substitute for it.

If you don't miss your life within, you are enough unto yourself. And only then are you beautiful. And only then you *are*.

Buddha said, "People cleave to their worldly possessions and selfish passions so blindly as to sacrifice their own lives for them. They are like a child who tries to eat a little honey smeared on the edge of a knife. The amount is by no means sufficient to appease his appetite, but he runs the risk of wounding his tongue."

Nothing is enough in this life to fulfill your desires, to fulfill your appetite. This world is a dream world—nothing can fulfill because only reality can be fulfilling. Have you watched? In a dream, you feel hungry in the night and in your dream you go to the fridge and open it and you eat to your heart's content. Of course, it helps in a way—it does not disturb your sleep; otherwise, the hunger will not allow you to sleep, you will have to wake up. The dream creates a substitute; you continue to sleep, you feel, "I have eaten enough." You have deceived your body. The dream is a deceiver. In the morning you will be surprised—you are still hungry—because a feast in the dream is equivalent to a fast. Feasting and fasting, both are the same in a dream because a dream is unreal. It cannot fulfill your hunger. To quench real thirst real water is needed. To fulfill you, a real-life reality is needed.

Buddha says you go on taking the risk of wounding yourself, but no fulfillment comes out of this life. Maybe here and there you have a taste of honey—sweet, but dangerous, unfulfilling. And the honey is smeared on the edge of a knife; there is every danger you will wound your tongue. Look at so many old people: You will not find anything else but wounds; their whole being is nothing but wounds and ulcers. When a person dies, you don't see blossoming flowers in his being; you see stinking wounds.

If a person has lived and not been deceived by his dreams and illusory desires, the older he grows the more beautiful he becomes. In his death he is superb. Sometimes you may come across an old man whose old age is more beautiful than his youth ever was. Then bow down before that old man—he has lived a true life, a life of inwardness, a life of "interiorness." Because if life is lived truly, then you go on becoming more and more beautiful and a grandeur starts coming to you, a grace. Something of the unknown starts abiding in your surroundings—you become the abode of the infinite, of the eternal. It has to be so because life is an evolution.

If when you are no longer young and you become ugly, that simply means in your youth you tasted honey on too many knives—you have become wounded. Now you will suffer cancerous wounds. Old age becomes a great suffering. And death is rarely beautiful, because rarely have people really lived. If a person has truly lived—like a flame burning from both ends—then his death will be a tremendous phenomenon, an utter beauty. You will see his life aglow when he is dying, at the maximum, at the optimum. In the last moment he will become such a flame; his whole life will become a concentrated perfume in that moment, a great luminosity will arise in his being. Before he leaves, he will leave behind him a memory.

That's what happened when Buddha left the world. That's what happened when Mahavira left the world. We have not forgotten them, not because they were great politicians or people of power—they were nobodies, but we cannot forget them. It is impossible to forget them. They had not done anything as far as history is concerned. We can almost omit them from history, we can leave them out of history and nothing will be lost. In fact, they never existed in the main current of history, they were by the side of it—but it is impossible to forget them. Their last moments have left a glory to humanity. Their last glow has shown us our own possibilities, our infinite potentialities.

SEEING AND BELIEVING

Buddha says again and again to his disciples, "Ihi passiko: come and see!" They are scientific people; Buddhism is the most scientific religion on the earth. Hence, it is gaining more and more ground in the world every day. As the world becomes more intelligent, Buddha will become more and more important. It is bound to be so. As more and more people come to know about science, Buddha will have great appeal, because he will convince the scientific mind—because he says, "Whatsoever I am saying can be practiced. And I don't say to you, 'Believe it,' I say, 'Experiment with it, experience it, and only then if you feel it yourself, trust it.' Otherwise there is no need to believe."

blowing out
the candle

IT IS SIGNIFICANT to understand that there is only one person, Gautam Buddha, who has used nothingness, emptiness, for the ultimate experience. All other mystics of the world have used fullness, wholeness, as the expression, the indication of the ultimate experience.

Why did Gautam Buddha choose a negative term? It is significant to understand—for your own spiritual growth, not for any philosophical reasons. I do not speak for philosophical reasons. I speak only when I see there is some existential relevance.

The idea of fullness, the idea of God, the idea of perfection, the idea of the absolute, the ultimate—all are positive terms. And Gautam Buddha was amazed to see the cunningness of human mind....

The innocent mystics have used the positive words because that was their experience. Why bother about the misery, which is no more? Why not say something about that which is now? The innocent mystics have spoken out of their "isness." But throughout the centuries the cunning minds of people around the world have taken advantage of it.

To the cunning mind, the idea of fullness, and the positive terms indicating it, became an ego trip: "I have to become God. I have to attain the absolute, the Brahma; I have to achieve the ultimate liberation." The "I" became the center of all our assertions. The trouble is that you cannot make the ultimate experience a goal for the ego. Ego is the barrier; it cannot become the bridge.

All the positive terms have been misused. Rather than destroying the ego, they have become decorations for the ego. God has become a goal; you have to achieve the goal. You become greater than God.

Remember, the goal cannot be greater than you. The achieved cannot be greater than the achiever. It is a very simple fact to understand.

All the religions have fallen because of this simple innocence of the mystics.

Gautam Buddha was the most cultured, the most educated, the most sophisticated person ever to become a mystic. There is no comparison in the whole of history. He could see where the innocent mystics had unknowingly given opportunities for cunning minds to take advantage. He decided not to use any positive term for the ultimate goal, in order to destroy the ego and any possibility of the ego taking any advantage.

He called the ultimate, nothingness, emptiness—*shunyata*, zero. Now, how can the ego make "zero" a goal? God can be made a goal but not zero. Who wants to become zero?—that is the fear. Everybody is avoiding all possibilities of becoming a zero, and Buddha made t an expression for the ultimate!

His word is *nirvana*.

He chose a tremendously beautiful word, but he shocked all the thinkers and philosophers by choosing the word *nirvana* as the most significant expression for the ultimate experience. *Nirvana* means "blowing out the candle."

Other mystics have said that you are filled with er ormous light, as if thousands of suns together have suddenly risen inside you, as if the sky full of stars has descended within your heart. These ideas appeal to the ego. The ego would like to have all the stars, if not inside the chest, then at least hanging on the coat outside the chest. "Enormous light"... the ego is very willing.

To cut the roots, Buddha says the experience is as if you were to blow out a candle. There was a small flame on the candle giving a small light—even that is gone, and you are surrounded with absolute darkness, abysmal darkness.

People used to say to him, "If you go on teaching such things, nobody is going to follow you. Who wants darkness, enormous darkness? You are crazy. You say that the ultimate experience is an ultimate death. People want eternal life, and you are talking about ultimate death?"

But he was a consistent man, and you can see that for forty-two years he hammered on the genius of the East without ever compromising with the ego. He also knows that what he is

cal ing darkness is too much light; that's why it looks like darkness. If one thousand suns rise in you, what do you think?—that you will feel enormous light? You will feel immense darkness, it will be too dazzling. Just look at one sun for a few seconds and you will feel your eyes are going blind. If one thousand suns are within you, inside the mind, the experience will be of darkness, not of light.

It will take a long time for you to get accustomed, for your eyes to become strong enough to see—slowly, slowly—darkness turning into light, death turning into life, emptiness turning into fullness. But he never talked about those things. He never said that darkness would ever turn into light. And he never said that death would become a resurrection at some later point, because he knows how cunning your ego is. If that is said, the ego will say, "Then there is no problem. Our aim remains the same; it is just that we will have to pass through a little dark night of the soul. But finally, we will have enormous light, thousands of suns."

Gautam Buddha had to deny that God existed—not that he was against God, a man like Gautam Buddha cannot be against God. And if Gautam Buddha is against God, then it is of no use for anybody to be in favor of God. His decision is decisive for the whole of humanity; he represents our very soul. But he was not against God. He was against the ego, and he was constantly careful not to give the ego any support to remain. If God can become a support, then there is no God.

One thing becomes very clear: although he used, for the first time, all negative terms, the man must have had tremendous charismatic qualities. He influenced millions of people. His philosophy is such that anyone listening to him would freak out. What is the point of all the meditations and all the austerities, renouncing the world, eating one time a day...and ultimately you achieve nothingness, you become zero! We are already better off than that—we may be miserable, but we *are* at least. Certainly, when you are completely a zero there cannot be any misery—zeros are not known to be miserable—but what is the gain?

Yet he convinced people, not through philosophy, but through his individuality, through his presence. He gave people the experience itself, so they could understand. It is emptiness as far as the world is concerned, it is emptiness for the ego, and it is fullness for the being.

There are many reasons for the disappearance of Buddha's thought from India, but this is one of the most significant. All other Indian mystics, philosophers, and seers have used positive terms. For centuries before Buddha, all of India was accustomed to thinking only in the positive; the negative was something unheard of. Under the influence of Gautam Buddha they followed him, but when he died his following started disappearing—because the following was not intellectually convinced; it was convinced because of his presence. Because of the eyes of Gautam Buddha they could see: "This man—if he is living in nothingness then there is no fear, we would love to be nothing. If this is where becoming a zero leads, if by being nothing such lotuses bloom in the eyes and such grace flows, then we are ready to go with this man. The man has a magic."

But his philosophy alone will not convince you, because it has no appeal for the ego.

Buddhism survived in China, in Ceylon, in Burma, in Japan, in Korea, in Indochina,

in Indonesia—in the whole of Asia except India—because the Buddhists who reached there dropped the negative terms. They started speaking in positive terms. Then the "ultimate," the "absolute," the "perfect"—the old terms returned. This was the compromise. So as far as I am concerned, Buddhism died with Gautam Buddha. Whatever exists now as Buddhism has nothing to do with Buddha because it has dropped his basic contribution, which was his negative approach.

I am aware of both traditions. I am certainly in a better position than Gautam Buddha was. Gautam Buddha was aware of only one thing—that the ego can use the positive.

And it is his great contribution, his courageous contribution, that he dropped the positive and insisted on the negative, emphasized the negative—knowing perfectly well that people were not going to follow this because it had no appeal for the ego.

To me, now both traditions are available. I know what happened to the positive—the ego exploited it. I know what happened to the negative. After the death of Gautam Buddha, the disciples had to compromise, compromise with the same thing which Gautam Buddha was revolting against.

So I am trying to explain both approaches together—emptiness as far as the world is concerned and fullness as far as the inner experience is concerned. This is a total approach, it takes note of both: that which has to be left behind, and that which is to be gained. All other approaches up to now have been half-and-half. Mahavira, Shankara, Moses, Mohammed, all used the positive. Gautam

> *If you think in terms of the sacred, you will find your life overflowingly full*

Buddha used the negative. I use both, and I don't see any contradiction. If you understand me clearly, then you can enjoy the beauty of both viewpoints. You need not be exploited by your ego or be afraid of death and darkness and nothingness. They are not two things. It is almost as if I were to put a glass of water in front of you, half-full and half-empty, and ask you whether the glass is empty or full. Either answer would be wrong, because the glass is both half-full and half-empty. From one side it is empty, from another side it is full.

Half of your life is part of the mundane world, the other half is part of the sacred. It is unfortunate, but there is no other way—we have to use the same language for both the mundane and the sacred

So one has to be alert. To choose the mundane will be missing something essential; if you think in terms of the mundane, you will find the sacred life empty. If you think in terms of the sacred, you will find it overflowingly full.